THE
VICTORIAN
HOME
IN CROSS STITCH

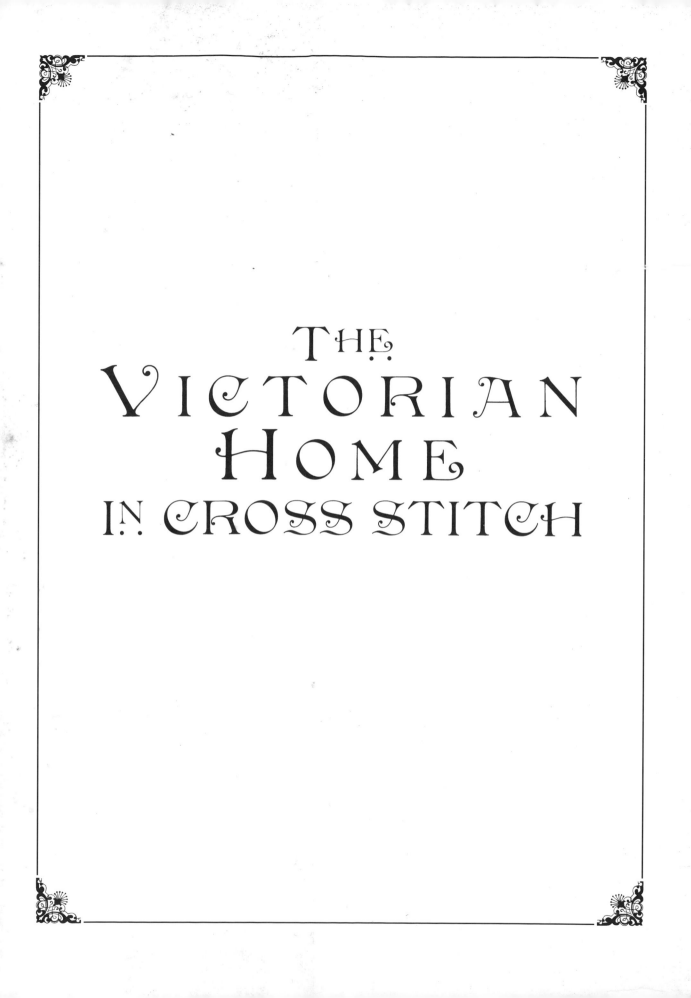

THE VICTORIAN HOME IN CROSS STITCH

Barbara Thompson
and Ann Green

David & Charles

· ACKNOWLEDGEMENTS ·

We wish to thank our families and friends for their support during the production of this book.
We would also like to thank Pam Ward at Huddersfield Picture Framing Company,
and Derick Armstrong, of Wickham, Tyne & Wear for framing all the pictures illustrated.

A DAVID & CHARLES BOOK

First published in the UK in 1996

Text and designs Copyright © Barbara Thompson & Ann Green 1996
Photography Copyright © Barbara Thompson & Ann Green and David & Charles 1996
Layout Copyright © David & Charles 1996

Barbara Thompson & Ann Green have asserted their right to be identified as the authors of
this work in accordance with the Copyright, Designs and Patents Act, 1988.

A catalogue record for this book is available from the British Library.

ISBN 07153 0430 5

Photography by Di Lewis
Book design by Diana Knapp
Typeset by GreenShires Icon, Exeter
and printed in Great Britain by Butler & Tanner Ltd
for David & Charles
Brunel House Newton Abbot Devon

·CONTENTS·

Introduction

Chapter One
THE DRAWING ROOM 8

Chapter Two
THE KITCHEN 28

Chapter Three
THE BEDROOM 48

Chapter Four
THE BATHROOM 62

Chapter Five
THE NURSERY 72

Chapter Six
ENTRANCE, HALL AND STAIRS 90

Chapter Seven
THE COMPLETE HOUSE WALL-HANGING 110

Chapter Eight
MATERIALS AND BASIC TECHNIQUES 118

Suppliers 127

Index 128

·INTRODUCTION·

Since Barbara and Ann formed a business partnership, manufacturing cross stitch embroidery kits, their designs have always been inspired by the home. Over the years they have designed many room settings, reflecting a variety of architectural styles, but for them, it is the grandeur and eclecticism of Victorian style which has always held the greatest appeal. Their inspiration for this, their second book, came from their love of Victoriana combined with their wish to produce a complete house design, consisting of all the elements which go to make up a home. In this book they have brought together many of the elaborate details of nineteenth-century architecture and interior design and translated them into cross stitch. Each chapter presents a room, which is complete and decorative in itself, but which can, if you wish, be added to the other room designs to build a grand house wall-hanging in the style of an open-fronted doll's house.

As well as the major room designs, each chapter is filled with smaller individual projects. These include many lovely gift ideas for you to make, from a tiny bookmark and pincushion to a more ambitious monogrammed night-dress case and a sumptuous woollen cushion. You are also given a glimpse of the inhabitants of the Victorian home and some insight into their life-style: from the elegant family enjoying Christmas entertainment, to the hard-working maid and gardener. Also, dotted throughout the book are some amusing sayings and poems designed for you to stitch. They are decorated in Victorian style, but, when displayed, are bound to add a humorous touch to any modern home.

The final chapter of the book is devoted to describing the materials used in the projects, and showing you how to tackle the various stitching techniques, so if you are a beginner this would be a good place for you to start. If you are already a competent stitcher, you may only need to dip into this chapter occasionally for hints on any aspect or technique that you are not sure of. Whatever your level of competence, as a beginner or an experienced cross-stitcher, Barbara and Ann feel sure that you will find lots of ideas in this book to inspire you to start stitching straight away.

THE ·DRAWING·ROOM·

·Chapter One·

The Victorians loved grandeur and show. Their drawing rooms, especially in the homes of the well-to-do, were furnished to show off their social status with elaborately carved mahogany furniture, heavy draperies and an abundance of pattern. The ladies of the household usually demonstrated their craft skills by turning their hand to a range of decorative arts; every available surface was covered with highly ornate decoration in rich colours.

Dark and deliberately ostentatious, the drawing room was rarely used during the week; being reserved for formal entertaining and as a place the family could 'withdraw' to for games, conversation and reading after church.

In this sumptuously ruched, draped and fringed example of a Victorian drawing room (pictured opposite) you'll find mahogany, velvet, brass, marble and cast iron, all solidly ornate.

· DRAWING · ROOM · PICTURE ·

The armchair, side table and clock are stitched in richly coloured threads and their bold shapes are typical of heavily carved mahogany. The button-back upholstery is authentic to the period and its buttons are created by just one cross stitch in black, outlined to give a solid circular effect. The padding is achieved by strong diagonal lines. The deep green thread and button-back effect gives that comfortable, plush velvet feel.

The footstool, covered in a more robust fabric, is also decorated with a tasselled edge. In the foreground the prettified table has two layers of covering. The folds of the lighter, ruched top cover, indicated by outline stitch, are held in place by fabric rosettes and the out-lining continues downwards to form the pleats of the under cover.

Since neither electricity nor gas has arrived in our drawing room, the only evening light is provided by oil lamp or candle. The candelabra here are given the effect of solid brass and the oil lamp features frosted glass and brass fittings.

The fireplace is a masterpiece of decoration. Its cast iron is moulded in an art nouveau style, the pattern illustrated in black back stitch over a lighter grey. The marble surround is suggested by the colour of thread and by using back stitch for the heavy carving at its base and mantle shelf. There is even a velvet mantle shelf cover complete with tassels.

Curtains were very dominant in Victorian drawing rooms. More decorative than practical, they were drawn only on the coldest evenings. Ours are typical in their use of heavy fabric and deep colour. The rich velvety look has been created by contrasting dark burgundy with a lighter pink to show how the fabric hangs in folds and catches the light; long rows of black outline stitch are used to indicate the three dramatic folds in its luxurious pleats.

Ornaments occupy all available surfaces. The background of walls and floor is stitched in alternate cross stitch (simply stitching a cross in every other square of the Aida fabric) in a rich colour to give the impression of flocked wallpaper and woollen carpet. Finally, below the window, the dado rail and carved panelling form a deep border around the walls of this grand yet very comfortable room.

- *Stitch count: 120 x 84*
- *Design size: 9 x 7in (23 x 18cm)*
- *14 x 12in (35.5 x 30cm) 14 count Aida fabric*
- *One skein of each colour of Anchor or DMC stranded cotton (floss) as listed in the colour key*

1 Before you start stitching, read through the preparation instructions on page 122 to find out how to mark the centre of your fabric.

2 Following the chart opposite, and starting either at the centre or if you prefer at the border, work all the cross stitch using two strands of thread. See the stitch instructions on page 122.

3 When you have completed the cross stitching, use one strand of thread to work the back stitch.

COLOUR KEY	ANCHOR	DMC
● Wine	70	915
\ Pink	895	223
V Off-white	830	3033
X Yellow	307	783
• Mahogany	351	400
+ Sandstone	373	437
‖ Dark grey	400	317
↑ Light grey	399	415
▽ Black	403	310
/ Dark green	879	500
□ Pale green	208	563
■ Dark brown	381	838

OUTLINES, WORKED IN BACK STITCH

Upper table cloth, mirror frame	Dark grey (400, 317)
Window, mirror, fire back, candles	Light grey (399, 415)
Blind, blind tassle, mantelpiece fringe, top of foot stool, lower table cloth, cushion	Wine (70, 915)
Picture frames, books, fireplace (except on grey), lamp, clock frame (not dial)	Dark brown (381, 838)
Bottom of foot stool, tassles on foot stool	Pink (895, 223)
Plant, plant pot	Dark green (879, 500)
Dog ornament, wood panelling	Mahogany (351, 400)
Candlestick	Yellow (307, 783)
All other outlines	Black (403, 310)

MOUNTING AND FRAMING

If you intend to frame this design as an individual picture, read the hints on page 125 for help with mounting and framing. If this picture is going to form part of the complete house, turn to page 110 for instructions on how to assemble the wall-hanging.

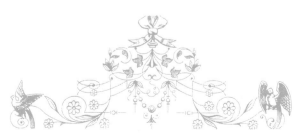

· FLORAL · CAMEO · BROOCHES ·

 The Victorian period was a time of great interest in all things spiritual and symbolic. Historically, flowers or precious stones in jewellery had been used to represent messages of love, fidelity and admiration to loved ones; remember how Shakespeare's Ophelia gave rosemary for remembrance and rue for grace.

The Victorians revived this lost art; many flowers took on secret and special meanings. Pansies said 'I am thinking of you', irises meant 'I have a message' and forget-me-nots stood for true love, and these examples,

Thrift and gentian brooches

THRIFT CHART

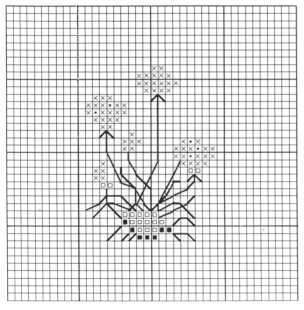

GENTIAN CHART

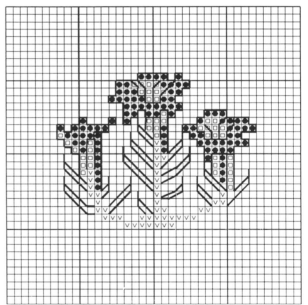

■ *Thrift stitch count: 24 x 18*

■ *Gentian stitch count: 27 x 21*

COLOUR KEY	ANCHOR	DMC
□ Green	208	563
X Pink	76	603
• Pale pink	48	963
■ Brown	373	437

OUTLINES, WORKED IN BACK STITCH
Stems and leaves   Green (208, 563)
Roots   Brown (373, 437)

COLOUR KEY	ANCHOR	DMC
● Medium blue	137	798
□ White	01	White
V Green	244	701

OUTLINES, WORKED IN BACK STITCH
Flowers   Dark blue (149, 336)
Leaves   Green (244, 701)

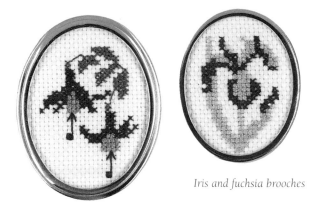

along with many others, were regularly used as motifs in stitched work.

Our six floral cameos have been especially designed to be decorative as well as symbolic and they are ideal for fitting into brooches, pendants, cards and a host of other, suitable items. All stitches are worked in one strand of thread, and we have suggested a 22 count Hardanger to ensure the motifs stay delicate and jewel-like when mounted in tiny brooches.

Iris and fuchsia brooches

- *Design size: 1 x 1½in (2.5 x 4cm)*
- *Materials required for each brooch design:*
- *3 x 2½in (7.5 x 6.5cm) 22 count Hardanger fabric*

- *One skein of each colour of Anchor or DMC stranded cottons (floss) as listed in the colour key*
- *1 x 1½in (2.5 x 4cm) brooch*

FUCHSIA CHART

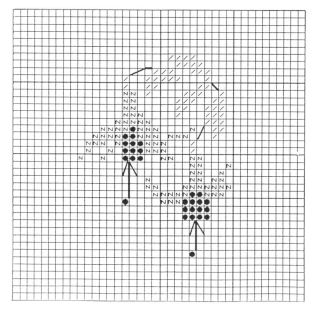

- *Fuchsia stitch count: 28 x 21*

COLOUR KEY		ANCHOR	DMC
N	Pink	76	603
●	Wine	70	915
/	Green	879	500

OUTLINES, WORKED IN BACK STITCH

Stems	Green (879, 500)
Stamens	Pink (76, 603)

IRIS CHART

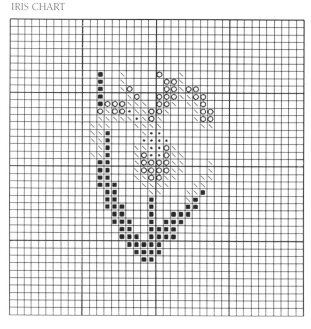

- *Iris stitch count: 26 x 17*

COLOUR KEY		ANCHOR	DMC
○	Light blue	130	799
\	Dark blue	149	336
■	Green	208	563
•	Yellow	307	783

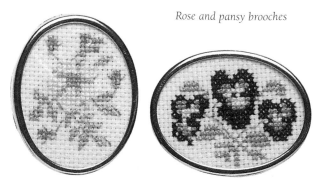

Rose and pansy brooches

1 Read the preparation instructions on page 122 to find out how to mark the centre of your fabric.
2 Following a chart from pages 12, 13 or 14, work all the cross stitch using one strand of thread. See the stitch instructions on page 122.

3 When you have completed the cross stitching, use one strand of thread to work the back stitch.

ASSEMBLING THE BROOCH
1 When you have completed the stitched design press out the back of the brooch and remove the enclosed piece of card. This will form the backing to your fabric.
2 . Place the card exactly over your stitched design and cut the fabric around the card. You should now have an oval piece of fabric exactly the same size as the card with your stitched design in the centre of it. Don't worry that your design comes close to the edge of the fabric. It won't fray once it's in the frame.
3 Re-assemble the brooch placing your fabric between the clear perspex front and the piece of card.

PANSY CHART

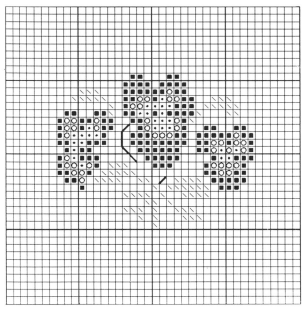

■ *Pansy stitch count: 27 x 21*

COLOUR KEY	ANCHOR	DMC
■ Purple	102	550
○ Mauve	109	210
• Yellow	300	745
\ Green	208	563

OUTLINES, WORKED IN BACK STITCH
Stems   Green (208, 563)

ROSE CHART

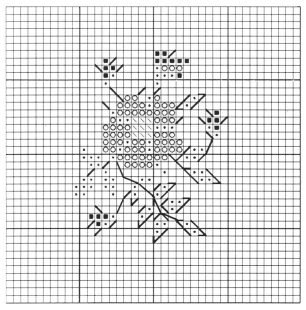

■ *Rose stitch count: 26 x 21*

COLOUR KEY	ANCHOR	DMC
○ Pale pink	48	963
■ Pink	895	223
• Green	208	563
/ Yellow	300	745

OUTLINES, WORKED IN BACK STITCH
Stems and leaves   Green (208, 563)

OTHER USES FOR FLORAL CAMEOS

You can use these six designs to decorate soft furnishings, napkins, handkerchiefs and towels as well as to create your own, special cards. Some of these ideas are illustrated on pages 16 and 17. On the two mats and the pillow case the floral designs have been stitched on to non-evenweave fabrics using a 14 count waste canvas. This method lets you work any cross stitch design on to a fine cotton or linen fabric which would otherwise not be suitable for evenweave work. The technique of using waste canvas is explained fully in the final chapter on page 119.

OVAL AND ROUND MATS

Plain mats, both oval and round, are readily available in haberdashery departments. See the Suppliers list on page 127. For the oval mat on pages 16 and 17, the pansy design has been used exactly as it appears on the chart, but it has been stitched on to a non-evenweave fabric using a 14 count waste canvas, so that each stitch works out bigger than in the brooch version. Use two strands of thread for the cross stitches, though for the back stitches one strand will do.

The rose design has been used on the round mat to add a little colour, possibly to tone with the decor of a room. Once again waste canvas has been used to translate this cross stitch design on to a fine linen fabric. See the full instructions for use of waste canvas on page 119. As with the pansy design on the oval mat, two strands of thread have been used for the cross stitches. Also, to fill out these larger stitches, diagonal half cross stitches have been used on the diagonal sides of the leaves rather than the simple back stitches in the brooch design. Diagonal half cross stitch technique is explained fully on page 123.

PILLOW CASE

Waste canvas lets you transfer a medley of flowers on to a plain white cotton pillow case. See full instructions on page 119. For our pillowcase on page 17, just above the red card, individual flowers have been selected from four of the cameo designs and assembled together almost at random. They overlap slightly here and there but they are still exact copies of the central rose, both fuchsias, the central pansy repeated twice, the left-hand pansy and the left-hand and central gentians.

LEAF BORDER CHART

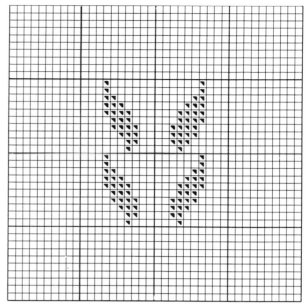

An easy way to compile a composite design like this is to trace or draw on to graph paper the flowers that you want to use and then cut them out individually. They can then be arranged and placed in a pleasing array before you start stitching. A pretty floral border can be created by repeating any of the flower designs and then adding an edging of leaves by using the chart above.

PINK CARD

The 3 x 2in (7.5 x 5cm) oval aperture of this card frames the rose design worked on an 18 count cream Aida fabric. To give a little more depth of colour, the pale pink has been completely substituted by medium pink (Anchor 895, DMC 223). Use one strand of thread throughout.

Overleaf These delightful motifs can be used in so many ways to decorate gifts and items for the home: (clockwise from top left) iris card; pansy card; pansy table mat; pansy brooch; pillow case featuring a composite floral motif; fuchsia card; fuchsia brooch; rose table mat; rose brooch; thrift card; rose card; gentian card; thrift brooch and gentian brooch

Choose one of six floral motifs to decorate a cameo brooch, or combine them to make a stunning picture

CREAM CARD

Here the thrift motif is worked with one strand of thread on 18 count cream Aida fabric. The card used in this case is a blank card without aperture.

First cut a piece of fabric slightly smaller than the card. When you have completed the floral motif, stitch a simple border, alternating crosses and single back stitches. Work the border on the sixth row in from the edge all round. Fray four rows of thread along each edge, leaving one row before the border.

Finally, attach the fabric to the card with a couple of pieces of double-sided sticky tape.

RED CARD

The 2³⁄₄in (7cm) aperture in this card left the fuchsia motif, worked on 18 count Aida, looking a little small. This is remedied and enhanced by a simple circle of crosses worked alternately in wine (Anchor 70, DMC 915) and dark green (Anchor 879, DMC 500).

BLUE CARD

The aperture in this card measures 4 x 3in (10 x 7.5cm), and so requires a bigger motif than the previous cards. The simplest way to enlarge a motif is to stitch it on to an Aida with larger squares, so we have used a cream 14 count fabric, and worked the design with two strands of thread.

The lower iris is exactly as depicted on the chart except that a brighter yellow has been used in the centre (Anchor 297, DMC 973).

The upper iris follows the design almost exactly but it is slightly overlapped by the lower one. To give a gentle colour contrast this flower has been stitched using two different coloured strands of thread at the same time. For the dark blue, one strand has been substituted by purple (Anchor 102, DMC 550). Similarly with the light blue, one strand has been replaced by mauve (Anchor 109, DMC 210).

GREEN CARD
Part of the pansy motif has been selected for the 2¾in (7cm) aperture in this card. The central pansy and part of the leaf design has been repeated four times, rotating the card at 90° each time it is repeated. The fabric used here is cream 14 count Aida.

· HOME · SWEET · HOME ·

Samplers were part of the way young girls learned to stitch in Victorian elementary schools and were produced as symbolic pictures where objects represented a life status or emotions. A popular addition to this tradition was the sampler which carried an improving proverb or moral, prettily presented to decorate the various rooms of the home. You will find several designs of this nature throughout the chapters of the book. Our 'Home Sweet Home' sampler fits this category. The message is simple and clear, but the lettering ornate and intricate.

In the Roman Ornamental alphabet we've used, each letter is differently and elaborately patterned. The outlines of the letters are quite solid and bold; the intricacy is within each letter's shape. You will notice that the colour range is quite restricted, centreing on rich burgundies and greens giving the effect of a highly decorated but harmonious piece. The message is dominant, confident and clearly communicated.

The close-up of the letter E opposite allows you to see clearly how the intricate patterning can be achieved quite simply with the varied use of cross stitch and diagonal half cross stitch. Dark green is used as the border colour in the E and as the outline colour for all the letters to give a continuity in drawing together the various patterns used on all the letters. The considerable use of diagonal half cross stitch in the E helps to give an almost three dimensional appearance to the main body of the letter. Notice that outlining has been used on the pale green pattern down the centre which gives it the illusion of being a twisted paper streamer, whereas the lack of outlining on the pink stitching helps to push the pink stitches into the background in relief to the pale green.

Added intricacy comes from interspersing the off-white stitches with the pink.

This kind of decoration is reminiscent of Roman mosaic designs and was much loved and mimicked by the Victorians.

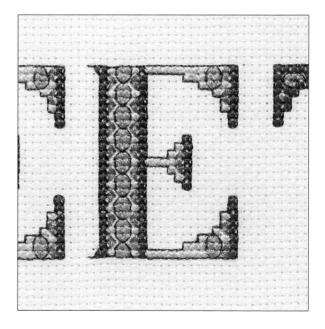

A single letter reveals the elaborate patterning of this alphabet

Overleaf A popular motto, the Home Sweet Home sampler offers a simple message in ornately decorated lettering (see page 20–21)

- *Stitch count: 142 x 130*
- *Design size: 11 x 9¹/₂in (28 x 24cm)*
- *17 x 15in (43 x 38cm) 14 count Aida fabric*
- *One skein of each colour of Anchor or DMC stranded cotton (floss) as listed in the colour key*

1 Before you start stitching, read through the preparation instructions on page 122 to find out how to mark the centre of your fabric.
2 Following the chart opposite, and starting at the centre, work all the cross stitch using two strands of thread. See the stitch instructions on page 122.
3 When you have completed the cross stitching, use one strand of thread to work the back stitch.
4 Finally, using one strand of thread, work the French knots following the stitch instructions on page 124.

MOUNTING AND FRAMING
Read the hints on page 125 for help with mounting and framing.

COLOUR KEY	ANCHOR	DMC
● Dark green	879	500
□ Olive green	846	936
○ Pale green	208	563
+ Pink	895	223
▽ Dark pink	896	3721
= Off-white	830	3033

OUTLINES, WORKED IN BACK STITCH
Pattern on W, central
  motif on H   Pink (895, 223)
Pattern on Os   Dark pink (896, 3721)
Surrounding of each letter,
  and all other outlines   Dark green (879, 500)

FRENCH KNOTS
Hs, Ms, S   Dark green (879, 500)
Corner motifs   Olive green (846, 936)
T   Off-white (830, 3033)

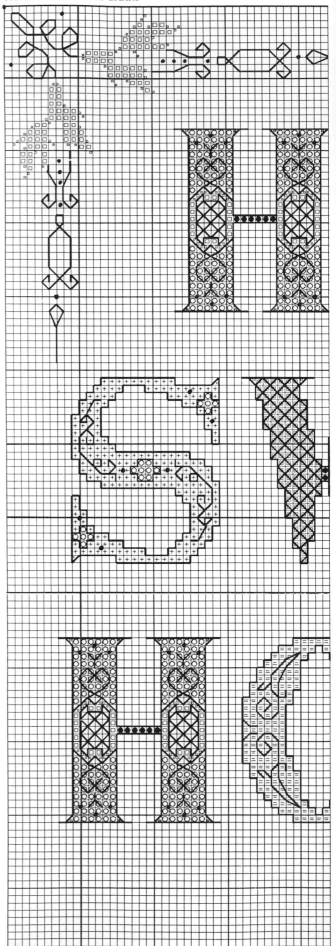

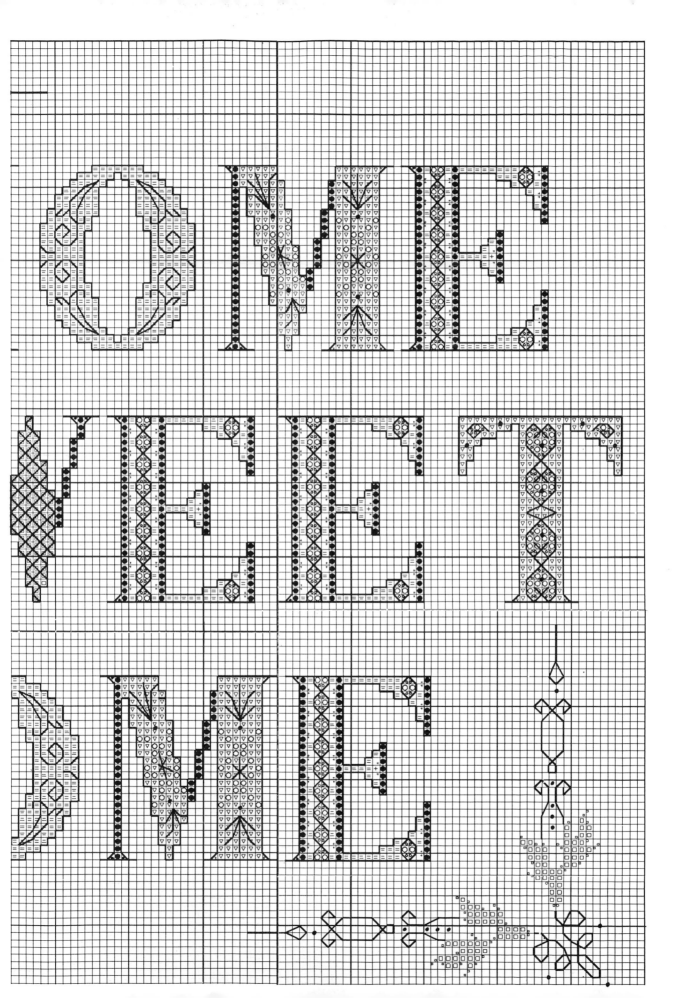

· CHRISTMAS · SCENE ·

The custom of bringing a fir tree into the house at Christmas time was introduced from Germany, and popularised by Prince Albert. So the family we show here are displaying the height of fashion and must be very proud to have such a hardy flourishing tree as the centrepiece of their decorated room.

We can suppose that this happy scene shows Christmas day, perhaps after luncheon, when excitement is high, but contained within the formality of domestic rituals. Mother, of course, is the epitome of grace and culture at the piano. Father, central in the picture, is the main authority within the family, and focus of the entertainment. Perhaps mother and children have been secretly practising this rendition for weeks and now offer their Christmas entertainment.

As this is a fashionable family, the children are both wearing sailor suits, very popular for boys and girls; in fact, a style that still represents gentility and social standing. Mother and father's clothes are late Victorian. There is a hint of a bustle in mother's dress, and father's wing collar and tight waistcoat with long dress coat indicate that the family is 'à la mode'.

There is a very limited range of colour used in this picture. Dark greens, greys, neutrals and dark reds are highlighted very slightly with gilt on the brass of the piano candelabra and on the candles in the tree. The result is restrained and sedate but, more importantly, authentic.

Again, we have used alternate cross stitch for the carpet and the ceiling border with just a suggestion of a pattern on the wallpaper.

The piano is the most solid area of cross stitch, relieved by the lighter trim around its various panels. You will notice that the keys slope to introduce perspective and that this is done cleverly in back stitch outline. Back stitch is also used to give the sharp edges to the children's and father's outfits, and it forms a mass of swirly shapes to create the many folds in mother's dress as she is seated at the piano.

The decorations are quite restrained and straightforward to stitch, being bold rather than fiddly. The tree is shaded in the more complex style needed to represent natural foliage. When stitching densely

patterned areas like the tree, where several colours are intermingled, it is easy to get a little lost. If you find that you are a stitch out here and there, don't worry unduly about correcting it, as the over-all effect will still be fine, and small deviations from the pattern will not be noticed in the finished picture.

❦

- Stitch count: 120 x 84
- Design size: 9 x 7in (23 x 18cm)
- 14 x 12in (35.5 x 30cm) 14 count Aida fabric
- One skein of each colour of Anchor or DMC stranded cotton (floss) as listed in the colour key

COLOUR KEY		ANCHOR	DMC
■	Dark brown	381	838
▽	Mahogany	351	400
S	Light brown	373	437
/	Grey/green	876	502
●	Dark green	879	500
↑	Peach	4146	3774
T	Dark pink	896	3721
X	Blue/grey	922	930
+	Dark grey	400	317
•	Light grey	399	415
○	Off-white	830	3033
U	White	01	White
‖	Gold		Cristallina or similar fine metallic thread (use three strands)

OUTLINES, WORKED IN BACK STITCH

Outline of children against the tree, presents, boy's clothes (except collar), man's clothes and hands, piano stool, shoes, woman's hair	Black (403, 310)
Baubles, star (use three strands)	Gold (Cristallina)
Woman's dress and necklace	Dark green (879, 500)
Facial details (except mouths), girl's hands	Dark grey (400, 317)
Mouths	Dark pink (896, 3721)
Girl's dress, boy's collar	Blue/grey (922, 930)
All other outlines	Dark brown (381, 838)

FRENCH KNOTS

Boy's jacket buttons	Light brown (373, 437)

CHRISTMAS SCENE CHART

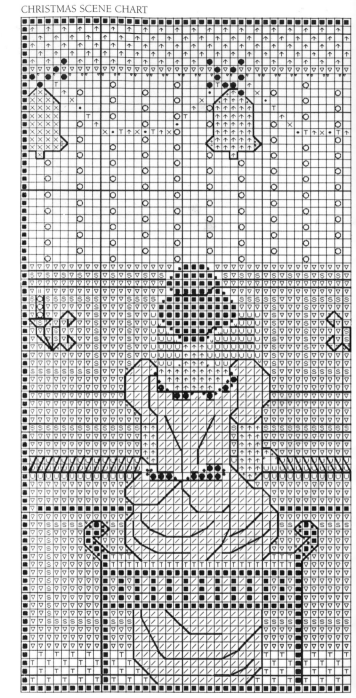

1 Before you start stitching, read through the preparation instructions on page 122 to find out how to mark the centre of your fabric.
2 Following the chart above, and starting either at the centre or if you prefer at the border, work all the cross stitch using two strands of thread, except for the gold thread which requires three strands.
See the stitch instructions on page 122.

3 When you have completed the cross stitching, use one strand of thread to work the back stitch except for the back stitch in gold thread which requires three strands.

4 And finally, to complete the Christmas scene, using one strand of thread, work the boy's buttons in French knots following the stitch instructions on page 124.

MOUNTING AND FRAMING

Read the hints on page 125 for help with mounting and framing. We have chosen a double mount picking out two colours from the design. Our ornate frame also helps to add to the special sense of occasion in this picture.

THE
·KITCHEN·
·Chapter Two·

Victorian and Edwardian kitchens were often gloomy places, not because of the lack of light or because the materials were dark, but because of an absence of colour. With their white tiled walls and large windows they were highly organised, serious places full of natural stone, wood, iron and glass; but colourless. Austere architectural lines were softened only by the detailed nature of cupboard and shelf contents. In contrast, of course, was the cooking range, with its warmly glowing fire providing a central focus whatever the weather outside.

· KITCHEN · PICTURE ·

In our kitchen design we have tried both to retain authenticity and create an attractive scene, so the colours introduced are subtle, soft and appropriate, with no strong primaries. The emphasis in the picture remains on natural materials in neutral colours, but with a light lemon yellow, a peachy tone and pale blues to warm the picture and create visual interest.

Placing plants on the windowsill and mantelshelf above the range is a good opportunity for introducing colour and variety of shape to what could otherwise be a dull symmetrical setting. It is these small details that charm, and there are many in this picture. The plate

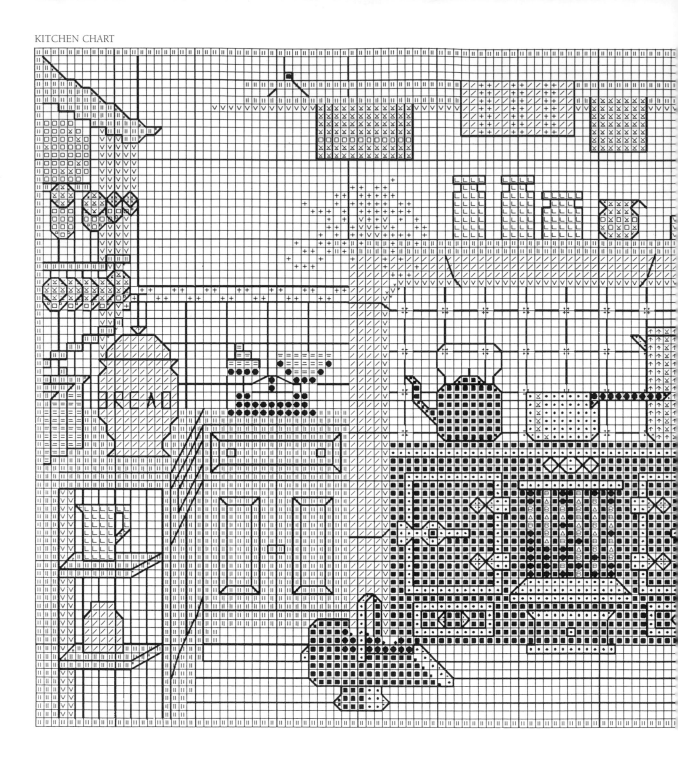

rack above the dresser is barely in the picture but gives the opportunity to colour the scene with blue crockery. The clothes rack is in itself a charming and nostalgic reminder of comfortable warm kitchens but also allows colour to be added in the towels and tea cloths hanging upon it.

Kettles and pans, bread crocks and stock pots have to be represented in the materials of the era but their inclusion and realism draw the eye. The tile border motif is appropriate to the Victorian period look, adding both pattern and colour, and the kitchen range, although stitched in grey, has intriguing door details and glowing coals within.

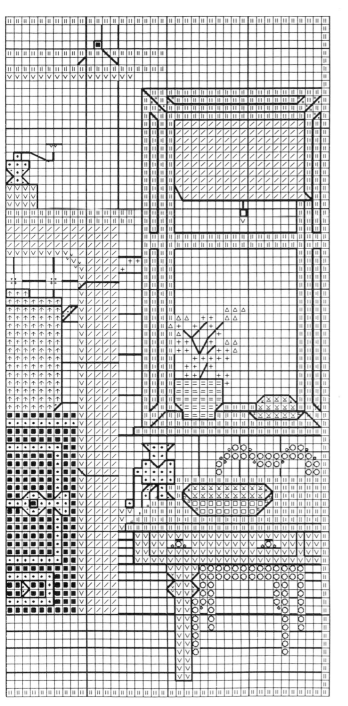

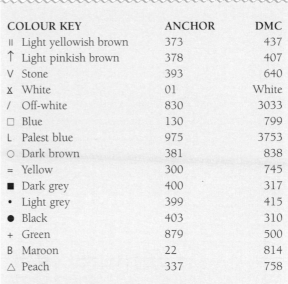

COLOUR KEY		ANCHOR	DMC
‖	Light yellowish brown	373	437
↑	Light pinkish brown	378	407
V	Stone	393	640
X	White	01	White
/	Off-white	830	3033
□	Blue	130	799
L	Palest blue	975	3753
○	Dark brown	381	838
=	Yellow	300	745
■	Dark grey	400	317
•	Light grey	399	415
●	Black	403	310
+	Green	879	500
B	Maroon	22	814
△	Peach	337	758

OUTLINES, WORKED IN BACK STITCH

Tiles	Light grey (399, 415)
Bolder tiles	Green (879, 500)
Floor, blind, off-white stone surround, large cooking pot, dresser behind cups, back wall of shelves, white towel, green striped towel	Stone (393, 640)
Blue cups, blue & white towel	Blue (130, 799)
Scales, range, kettle, pan	Black (403, 310)
Cupboards, shelves, window surrounds, stone surround, table, yellow pots	Dark brown (381, 838)
All other outlines	Dark grey (400, 317)

1 Before you start stitching, read through the preparation instructions on page 122 to find out how to mark the centre of your fabric.
2 Following the chart above, and starting at the centre or if you prefer at the border, work all the cross stitch using two strands of thread. See the stitch instructions on page 122.
3 When you have completed the cross stitching, use one strand of thread to work the back stitch.

MOUNTING AND FRAMING

If you intend to frame this design as an individual picture, read the hints on page 125 for help with mounting and framing. If this picture is going to form part of the complete house, turn to page 110 for instructions on how to assemble the wall-hanging.

- *Stitch count: 120 x 84*
- *Design size: 7 x 9in (18 x 23cm)*
- *12 x 14in (30 x 35.5cm) 14 count Aida fabric*
- *Two skeins light yellowish brown stranded cotton (floss) (Anchor 373, DMC 437)*
- *One skein of each of the other colours of stranded cotton (floss) as listed in the colour key*

· THE · CONSERVATORY ·

This splendid structure in glass, brick and wrought iron would accommodate plants for show throughout the year and be a less formal sitting and entertaining space, or an alternative to the garden during inclement weather. It would be used then as now in fact.

Our conservatory has vast areas of glass roof stitched in alternate cross stitch in the palest silvery blue. The wrought iron edging is worked in a single strand of back stitch, and a variety of colours is introduced in the stained glass sections and in the flowers around the outside. The solid base and rectangular shape of the conservatory are typically Victorian and can be seen in many contemporary reproductions.

- *Stitch count: 131 x 109*
- *Design size: 9 x 8in (23 x 20cm)*
- *14 x 13in (35.5 x 33cm) 14 count Aida fabric*
- *One skein of each colour of stranded cotton (floss) as listed in the colour key*

1 Before you start stitching, read through the preparation instructions on page 122 to find out how to mark the centre of your fabric.
2 Following the chart on pages 34 and 35, and starting at the centre, work all the cross stitch using two strands of thread. See the stitch instructions on page 122.
3 When you have completed the cross stitching, use one strand of thread to work the back stitch.

MOUNTING AND FRAMING
Read the hints on page 125 for help with mounting and framing.

CONSERVATORY CHART

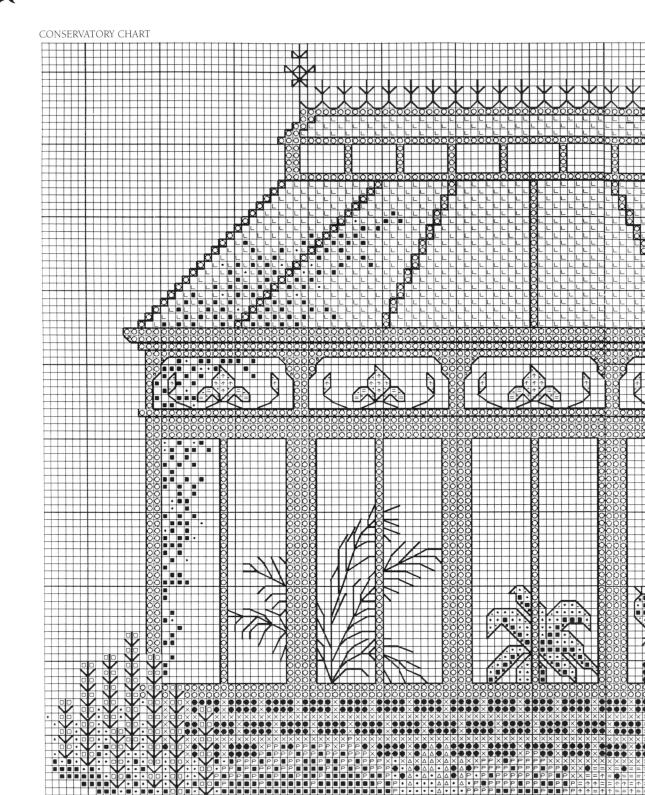

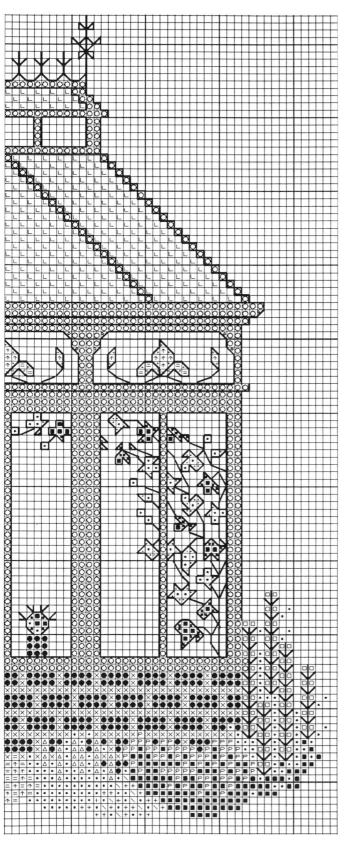

COLOUR KEY	ANCHOR	DMC
○ White	01	White
□ Purple	102	550
P Mauve	109	210
+ Light blue	130	799
S Medium blue	137	798
L Palest blue	975	3753
= Light green	241	704
• Medium green	244	701
■ Dark green	879	500
△ Yellow	300	745
X Light grey	399	415
↑ Pink	895	223
● Brick	5975	356

OUTLINES, WORKED IN BACK STITCH

Plants outside conservatory	Medium green (244, 701)
Plants inside conservatory	Dark green (879, 500)
Conservatory	Dark grey (400, 317)

THE KITCHEN GARDEN

A house of this size would have had a kitchen garden to provide for the family and their guests. This would have been a practical working site with rows of vegetables, fruits and herbs, with the gardener and possibly his lad to plan, prepare and harvest the crop year round.

We have found that there are too few tokens or tributes that can be stitched for men, but in this chapter, with its touches of humour, several designs may fit the bill.

· VEGETABLE · SAMPLER ·

Our Vegetable Sampler is resplendent with garden vegetables in bright reds, greens, purple and gold stitched, as if planted, in regular rows across the fabric. The border is a delicate arch of bright green and red climbing beans rising from an orange pumpkin and its trailing dark green leaves. Each vegetable motif is solid and easy to cross stitch with just a little back stitch outlining to crisp its shape and definition. This original sampler has a space for the date or could be personalised with garden mottoes or a name or address, and would make a perfect gift for a keen vegetable gardener. This is our first example of a cross stitch picture that may be given to a man, perhaps as a gesture of appreciation. We are not assuming that all vegetable gardeners are men however!

- *Stitch count: 200 x 165*
- *Design size: 15 x 12in (38 x 30cm)*
- *20 x 17in (51 x 43cm) 14 count Aida fabric*
- *Two skeins each of dark green (Anchor 879, DMC 500) and medium green (Anchor 244, DMC 701)*
- *One skein of each of the other colours of stranded cotton (floss) as listed in the colour key*

1 Before you start stitching, read through the preparation instructions on page 122 to find out how to mark the centre of your fabric.
2 Following the chart on pages 38 and 39, and starting at the centre, work all the cross stitch using two strands of thread. See the stitch instructions on page 122.
3 When you have completed the cross stitching, use one strand of thread to work the back stitch.
4 The space at the top centre of the border can be used either for your initials or for the date. Numbers are included on the Vegetable Sampler chart, and letters can be selected from the alphabets on pages 82 and 85. Draw in the numbers or letters you want to use on the chart so you can centre them before you start to stitch.

MOUNTING AND FRAMING
Read the hints on page 125 for help with mounting and framing. We suggest the use of a light wood frame which tones with modern pine and oak kitchens.

VEGETABLE MINIATURES

The individual vegetable designs can be put to a variety of uses as decoration for kitchen linen such as tea towels, napkins, oven-gloves etc. Here we have stitched six designs on to linen napkins, using waste canvas to transfer the cross stitch design on to a non-evenweave fabric. The technique for using waste canvas is fully explained in the last chapter on page 119.

- *Design size: approximately 2 x 2in (5 x 5cm)*
- *Materials required for each napkin:*
- *One cotton or linen napkin for each design*
- *One skein of each colour of Anchor or DMC stranded cotton (floss) as listed in the colour key. See the Suppliers list on page 127 for further information*
- *One piece of 14 count waste canvas measuring 3 x 3in (7.5 x 7.5cm) for each design*

1 Before you start stitching, read through the instructions on page 119 showing you how to use waste canvas, and tack (baste) your waste canvas to the napkin as described.
2 Following the chart of the vegetable you require, and starting at the centre, work all the cross stitch using two strands of thread. See the stitch instructions on page 122.
3 When you have completed the cross stitching, use one strand of thread to work the back stitch.
4 Following the instructions on page 119, use tweezers to carefully remove the waste canvas one thread at a time.

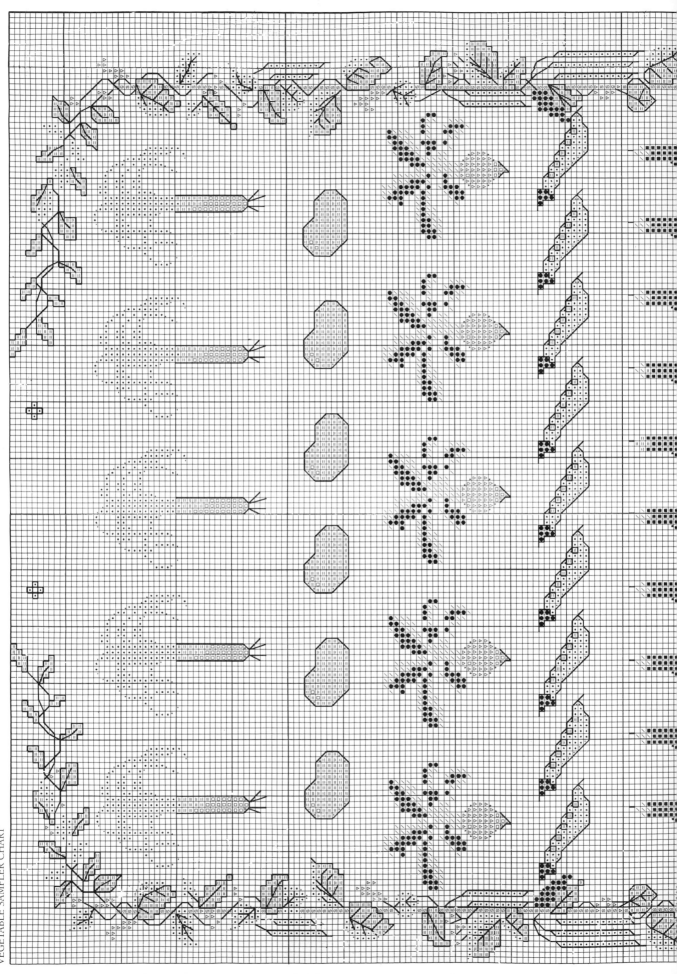

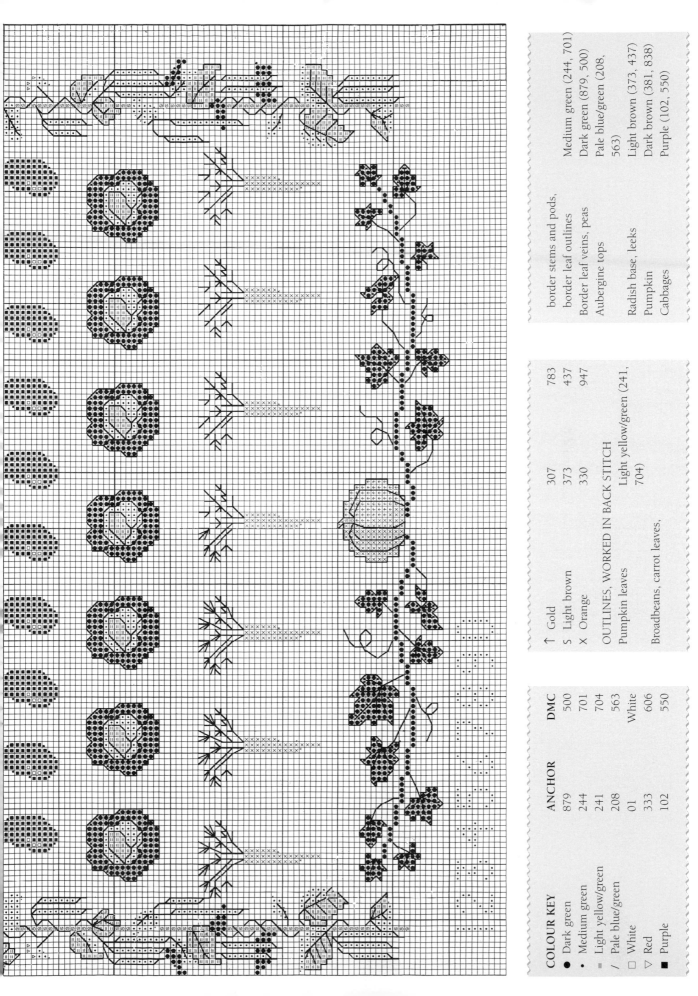

border stems and pods,
border leaf outlines   Medium green (244, 701)
Border leaf veins, peas   Dark green (879, 500)
Aubergine tops   Pale blue/green (208, 563)
Radish base, leeks   Light brown (373, 437)
Pumpkin   Dark brown (381, 838)
Cabbages   Purple (102, 550)

↑ Gold   307   783
S Light brown   373   437
X Orange   330   947

OUTLINES, WORKED IN BACK STITCH
                           Light yellow/green (241, 704)
Pumpkin leaves

Broadbeans, carrot leaves,

COLOUR KEY		ANCHOR	DMC
●	Dark green	879	500
•	Medium green	244	701
=	Light yellow/green	241	704
/	Pale blue/green	208	563
□	White	01	White
▽	Red	333	606
■	Purple	102	550

PEAS CHART

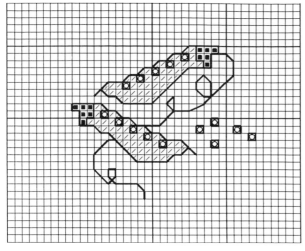

■ *Peas stitch count: 25 x 21*

COLOUR KEY	ANCHOR	DMC
■ Dark green	879	500
/ Medium green	244	701
○ Light yellow/green	241	704

OUTLINES, WORKED IN BACK STITCH
All outlines   Dark green (879, 500)

RED PEPPER CHART

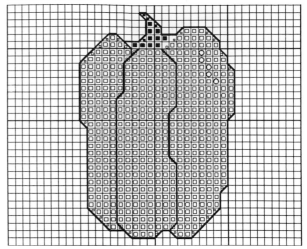

■ *Red pepper stitch count: 31 x 21*

COLOUR KEY	ANCHOR	DMC
□ Red	9046	321
■ Medium green	244	701
○ White	01	White

OUTLINES, WORKED IN BACK STITCH
All outlines   Dark green (879, 500)

LEEK CHART

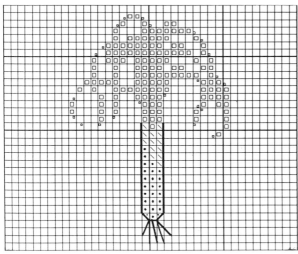

■ *Leek stitch count: 31 x 22*

COLOUR KEY	ANCHOR	DMC
□ Medium green	244	701
\ Light yellow/green	241	704
• White	01	White

OUTLINES, WORKED IN BACK STITCH
All outlines   Light brown (373, 437)

CARROT CHART

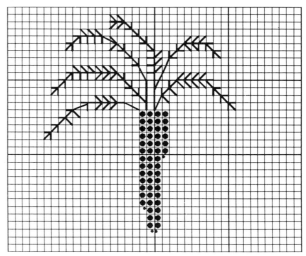

■ *Carrot stitch count: 30 x 26*

COLOUR KEY	ANCHOR	DMC
● Orange	330	947

OUTLINES, WORKED IN BACK STITCH
Leaves   Medium green (244, 701)

*Opposite A set of linen napkins can make a perfect gift
for a gardener*

RADISH CHART

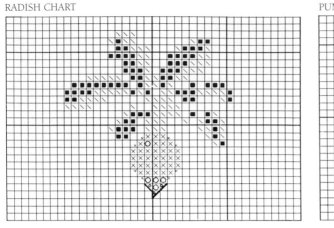

■ *Radish stitch count: 23 x 23*

COLOUR KEY	ANCHOR	DMC
■ Dark green	879	500
\ Pale blue/green	208	563
X Red	9046	321
O White	01	White

OUTLINES, WORKED IN BACK STITCH
Base of radish | Light brown (373, 437)

PUMPKIN CHART

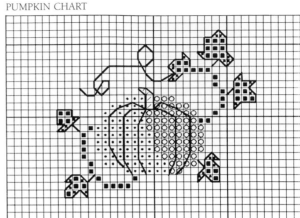

■ *Pumpkin stitch count: 26 x 23*

COLOUR KEY	ANCHOR	DMC
■ Dark green	879	500
• Gold	307	783
O Orange	330	947
/ Brown	351	400

OUTLINES, WORKED IN BACK STITCH
Leaves and stems | Dark green (879, 500)
Pumpkin | Brown (351, 400)

· THE · GARDENER ·

 Our gardener stands in front of his territory, his greenhouse. This has the look of a pavilion with a rather elegant porch. He stands formally dressed in waistcoat and tie. As pictures of the time confirm, these would be his working clothes. We have tried to make the man look dignified and very much part of the household.

■ *Stitch count: 90 x 50*
■ *Design size: 4 x 7in (10 x 18cm)*
■ *8 x 11in (20 x 28cm) 14 count Aida fabric*
■ *One skein of each colour of Anchor or DMC stranded cotton (floss) as listed in the colour key*

1 Before you start stitching, read through the preparation instructions on page 122 to find out how to mark the centre of your fabric.
2 Following the chart on page 44, and starting either at the centre or if you prefer at the border, work all the cross stitch using two strands of thread. See the stitch instructions on page 122.
3 When you have completed the cross stitching, use one strand of thread to work the back stitch, except for the dark grey outline of the cloche which requires two strands.

MOUNTING AND FRAMING
Read the hints on page 125 for help with mounting and framing.

THE GARDENER CHART

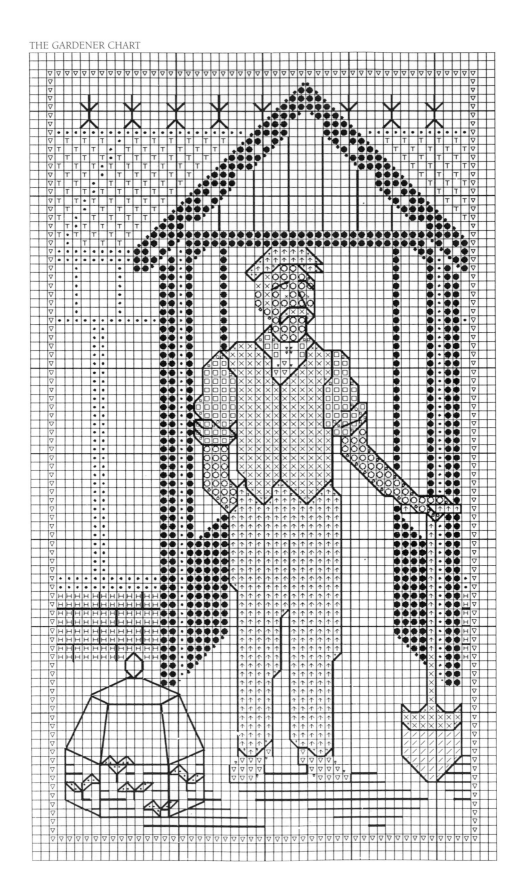

COLOUR KEY	ANCHOR	DMC
X Dark grey	400	317
/ Light grey	399	415
○ Light yellowish brown	373	437
H Brick	340	919
T Palest blue	975	3753
▽ Dark brown	381	838
↑ Stone	393	640

	ANCHOR	DMC
• Medium green	244	701
● Dark green	879	500
□ White	01	White

OUTLINES, WORKED IN BACK STITCH

Greenhouse structure	Medium green (244, 701)
Cloche (use two strands)	Dark grey (399, 415)
All other outlines	Dark brown (381, 838)

• GARDENING • PROVERB •

We dare not attribute this to the Victorians and suspect that it is a contemporary American witticism. However, we have presented this saying in the style of commemorative and improving messages of the age, and hope it convinces! The trailing interwoven ivy motif and the fine upright script with sober colours confer a dignity which belies the message. Projects such as this are relatively quick to stitch and are perfect when you need a stylish present in a hurry.

GARDENING PROVERB CHART (KEY ON PAGE 46)

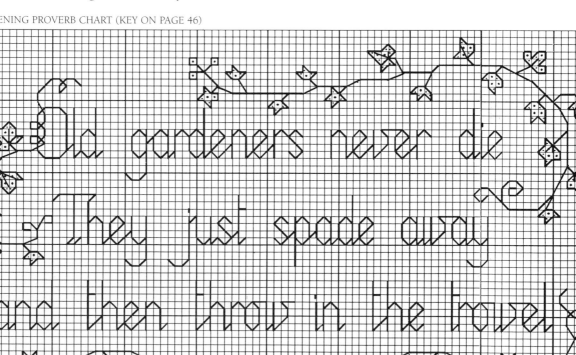

Gardening proverb picture

GARDENING PROVERB CHART ON PAGE 45

COLOUR KEY	ANCHOR	DMC
• Light green	241	704

OUTLINES, WORKED IN BACK STITCH
Proverb lettering (use two strands), author's name	Maroon (22, 814)	
All other outlines	Dark green (879, 500)	

- *Stitch count: 91 x 52*
- *Design size: 7 x 4in (18 x 10cm)*
- *11 x 8in (28 x 20cm) 14 count Aida fabric*
- *One skein of each colour of Anchor or DMC stranded cotton (floss) as listed in the colour key*

1 Before you start stitching, read through the preparation instructions on page 122 to find out how to mark the centre of your fabric.

2 Following the chart on page 45, and starting at the centre, use two strands of thread to work the words of the proverb in back stitch.

3 Using one strand of thread, work the author's name in back stitch.

4 Using one strand of thread, work the ivy stems in back stitch.

5 Using two strands of thread, work the ivy leaves in cross stitch.

6 Finally, use one strand of thread to complete the outlining of the leaves.

MOUNTING AND FRAMING

Read the hints on page 125 for help with mounting and framing. Notice that for this small design we have gone to town with a double mount, picking out the maroon and green colours from the picture. For a less elaborate surround, the picture could look equally charming without a mount in a simple wooden frame selected to tone with a particular decor.

THE · BEDROOM ·
Chapter Three

The privacy of a fully curtained bed was essential in grand homes before Victoria's time, when houses were built without corridors, and people had to pass through one room to reach the next. During the nineteenth century however, architectural styles changed as a new enthusiasm grew for a healthier domestic environment. The four poster gave way to the half-tester, which was draped only around the head, giving a more airy sleeping space. Windows were left open at night wherever possible, and a bedroom fireplace was considered essential to help provide a through-draught. A high ceiling was also a necessary feature in the provision of fresh air. A folding screen was often carefully placed near the bed to afford some privacy from the door, and this also helped to exclude excessive draughts in winter.

· BEDROOM · PICTURE ·

Our light and airy, high ceilinged bedroom features furnishings in burgundy and green, the key colours of the most formal rooms, and the decor reflects the many revivalist styles of the era.

The dark varnished wooden furniture and elaborately carved bed panel clearly reflect the classical revival of the time. We achieve these effects by

COLOUR KEY		ANCHOR	DMC
■	Dark brown	381	838
↑	Light brown	373	437
/	Mahogany	351	400
□	Medium pink	895	223
+	Dark pink	896	3721
B	Wine	70	915
•	White	01	White
○	Pale blue	975	3753
X	Green	208	563

OUTLINES, WORKED IN BACK STITCH

Screen, drapes, light shades	Wine (70, 915)
Pillows, wall behind pillows	Medium pink (895, 223)
Bedspread, jug and bowl, jars, vase	Blue/grey (922, 930)
Flowers in picture	Green (208, 563)
All other outlines	Dark brown (381, 838)

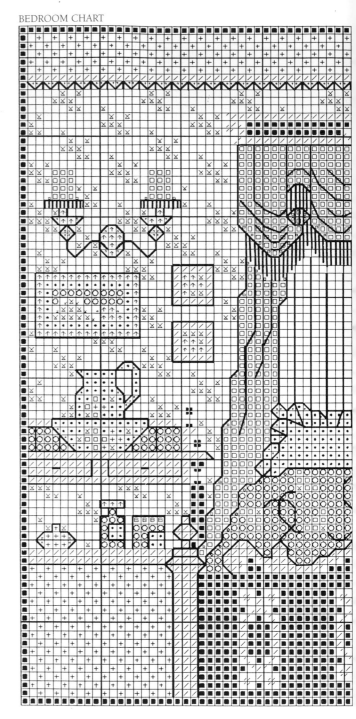

contrasting very dark brown with a rich mahogany colour, and using a combination of outlining and half cross stitch to show the pattern relief.

This classical style is also seen in the half-tester bed, centrally placed, and headed with folded and ruched sumptuous velvet drapery. Long outline stitches worked in parallel, half a stitch apart, represent the heavy fringing.

The bed cover design is Jacobean in origin, and the screen has an art nouveau look, yet another style current by the end of the Victorian era. Other touches of elegance are achieved by the addition of gilt or mahogany framed pictures, a wash stand displaying jars and potion bottles, and pottery decorated with flowers.

The carpeted floor and textured ceiling have been worked once again in alternate cross stitch to give a diffuse background.

Between the flock wallpaper and the painted ceiling we have used an egg-and-dart edging design, a popular style throughout the period. This is a sequence of oval and pointed shapes (eggs and darts!) moulded in the plasterwork or carved into the woodwork. We have depicted this design simply with half cross stitches and appropriate outlining.

- *Stitch count: 120 x 84*
- *Design size: 9 x 7in (23 x 18cm)*
- *14 x 12in (35.5 x 30cm) 14 count Aida fabric*
- *One skein of each colour of Anchor or DMC stranded cotton (floss) as listed in the colour key*

1 Before you start stitching, read through the preparation instructions on page 122 to find out how

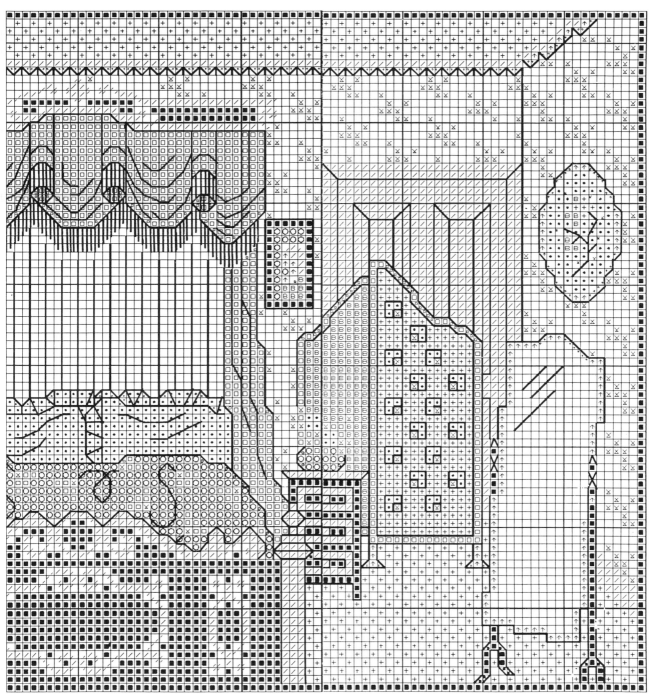

to mark the centre of your fabric.

2 Following the chart above, and starting either at the centre or if you prefer at the border, work all the cross stitch using two strands of thread. See the stitch instructions on page 122.

3 When you have completed the cross stitching, use one strand of thread to work the back stitch. Work the bed fringing as single long stitches, half a stitch apart.

MOUNTING AND FRAMING

If you intend to frame this design as an individual picture, read the hints on page 125 for help with mounting and framing. If this picture is going to form part of the complete house, turn to page 110 for instructions on how to assemble the wall-hanging.

· CUSHION ·

 Taking the design from the screen in the bedroom scene, here we have extended the use of cross stitch to wool (yarn) and canvas. Although the stitch instructions are exactly the same as for stranded cotton (floss) and Aida fabric, you will find it quite a different medium in which to work. We give more information on how to set about this type of project on page 121.

The joy of this design is that it has a very simple repeating pattern, which can easily be adapted to suit any size of cushion at all, from a pin cushion to a large floor cushion. There is no top or bottom to the design, but to prevent confusion, we will talk about the design as it appears on the chart on pages 54 and 55. It consists of a series of long chains, each with square motifs alternating to left and right along its length. It may be useful to colour in the chains and motifs on the chart.

The length you make each chain will determine the length of your cushion. The number of chains that you put side by side will determine the width. In our standard size cushion we have seven motifs along each chain, and four chains side by side, thus making an almost square cushion.

- *Stitch count: 146 x 143*
- *Design size: 14¹/₂ x 14¹/₂in (37 x 37cm)*
- *22 x 22in (56 x 56cm) 10 count interlock canvas, or the nearest to that width that the shop sells*
- *Paterna or Anchor tapestry wool (yarn) in the colours listed in the colour key. Buy the background colour wool (yarn) in a large hank, and the other colours in normal skeins. Start with three skeins of light pink and six skeins each of the rest. Then buy more if necessary*
- *20in (50cm) of backing material, such as a sturdy cotton, in a colour to tone with the cross stitch. We chose a rich plum colour*
- *2¹/₄yd (2m) of piping for the edging of the cushion. This can be bought in a toning colour, or you can make your own by covering piping cord with extra backing material cut on the cross*
- *One 15 x 15in (38 x 38cm) cushion pad*

1 Attach the piece of canvas to your frame, according to the frame instructions. See the Suppliers list on page 127 for information on frames.
2 Cut a length of wool (yarn) with which to start stitching. Some tapestry wool (yarn), such as Paterna, is made up of three strands, which you would normally use if working the cushion in tent stitch. But, as we are using cross stitch, it is only necessary to use two strands of wool (yarn) at a time. So separate out two strands, leaving the third strand to match up with another strand from a different cut length. Other wool (yarn), such as Anchor, does not separate into strands and should be used as it comes. See further information on the use of wool (yarn) in Chapter Eight.
3 Using two strands of the background colour, make your first row of 146 cross stitches across the top of the canvas leaving a 4in (10cm) gap at the top of the canvas (including the part of the canvas that is stitched to the frame), and a 4in (10cm) gap down the side at which you start to stitch.
4 Complete the top border by stitching two more rows beneath the first one.
5 In the same colour, stitch in the two side borders of three rows each, making sure that you have 143 stitches in each row.
6 Follow the chart on pages 54 and 55 to work the pattern of chains and motifs.
7 Fill the remaining space with background colour.
8 Stitch three rows across to make the bottom border.

MAKING UP
1 Remove your design from its frame. It should not need stretching or pressing as cross stitch has an even tension.
2 Cut down the border of canvas to leave about 1in (2.5cm) all round, so that the canvas measures about 16¹/₂in (42cm).
3 Cut out two pieces of backing material, one measuring 16¹/₂ x 13in (42 x 33cm), and the other measuring 16¹/₂ x 10in (42 x 25.5cm).
4 Machine hem along *one* 16¹/₂in (42cm) edge of each backing piece.

COLOUR KEY		ANCHOR	PATERNA
■	Plum	8422	A910
•	Medium pink	8418	A912
=	Light pink	8482	A915
□	White	8002	A263
X	Green	8966	D502

5 Pin the piping on to the right side of the canvas all around the cross stitching, with the raw edges facing outwards. Tack (baste) it into place sewing as closely as possible to the cross stitching.

6 Place the two backing pieces overlapping and right sides down on to the right side of the canvas, as shown in Fig 1.

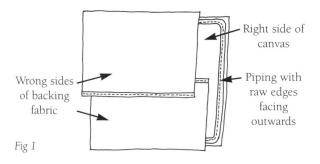

Wrong sides of backing fabric

Right side of canvas

Piping with raw edges facing outwards

Fig 1

7 Align all the side edges, and pin or tack (baste) them together before machine stitching along the four sides keeping as close as possible to the cross stitching. You may even stitch slightly on to the outer edge of cross stitching. See Fig 2. You may find that an ordinary machine needle is not strong enough to stitch through the canvas, but your specialist sewing machine supplier will be able to provide you with a suitable needle.

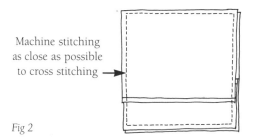

Machine stitching as close as possible to cross stitching

Fig 2

8 Turn the cushion right side out and stuff with a cushion pad.

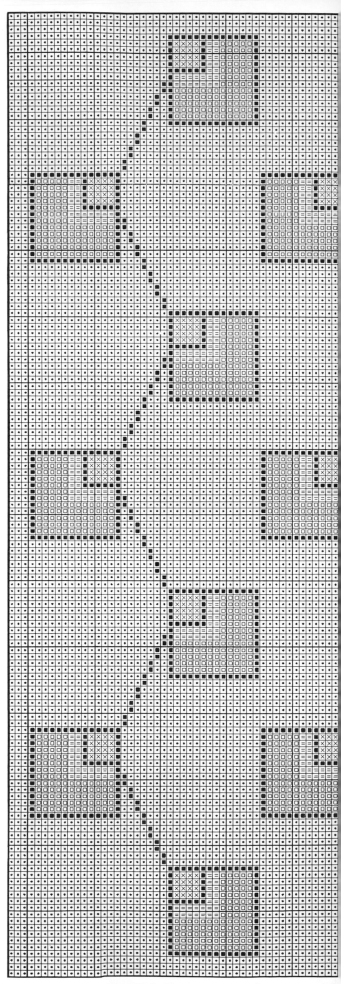

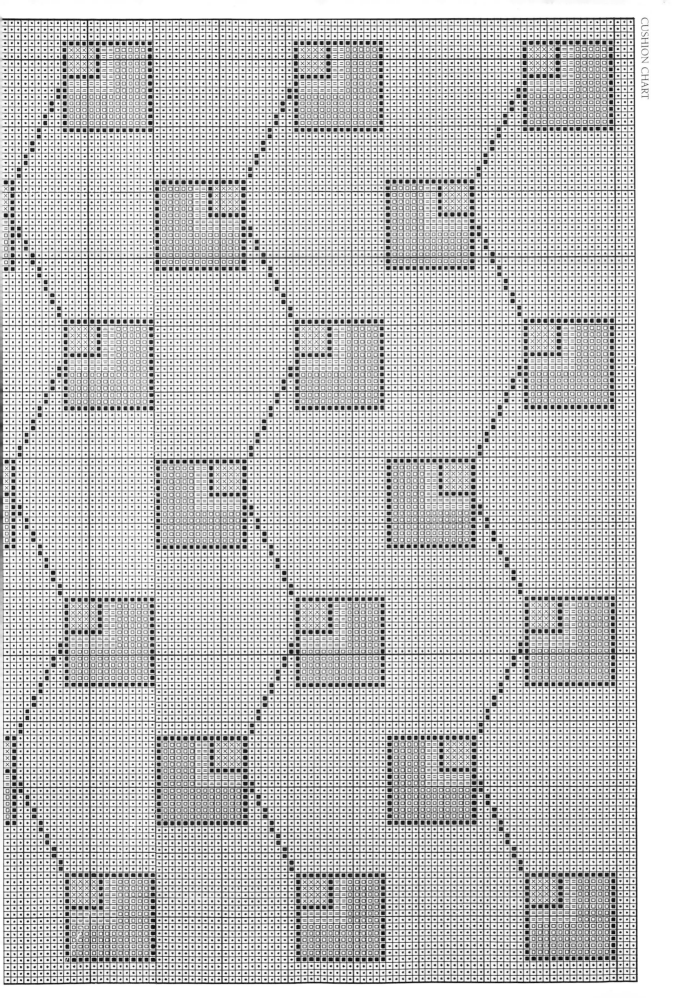

· BOOKMARK ·

The stylised carnation design used on this bookmark has been taken from the Jacobean bedspread in the bedroom design, and is also reminiscent of the carnation seen on many samplers. In the symbolism of samplers, the pink carnation represents maternal love, making this a lovely gift idea from mother to daughter or vice versa.

The bookmark can either be made using a piece of evenweave edging ribbon (see Suppliers list on page 127), as illustrated here, or you can improvise, using a left-over piece of Aida which can be frayed. Work the design, and then trim to six rows from the outer edge of the border. Carefully fray the Aida along each edge, having one row before the border.

- *Stitch count: 123 x 25*
- *Design size: 8 x 1½in (20 x 4cm)*
- *10in (25.5cm) cream evenweave edging ribbon, 2in (5cm) wide*
- *One skein of each colour of Anchor or DMC stranded cotton (floss) as listed in the colour key*
- *9in (23cm) cream petersham ribbon, 1½in (4cm) wide*

1 Before you start stitching, read through the preparation instructions on page 122 to find out how to mark the centre of the evenweave ribbon.
2 Following the chart below, and starting either at the centre or if you prefer at the border, work all the cross stitch using two strands of thread. See the stitch instructions on page 122.
3 When you have completed the cross stitching, use one strand of thread to work the back stitch.

MAKING UP
1 Cut the evenweave ribbon to within ½in (1.25cm) of the border at each end, and turn under a small hem leaving two rows of evenweave next to the cross stitch border. Pin or tack (baste) the hem.
2 Cut and hem the petersham ribbon in the same way, leaving it ¼in (5mm) shorter than the evenweave ribbon.
3 With wrong sides together, pin or tack (baste) the two ribbons together, and then stitch them together all round using a small neat hemming stitch.

COLOUR KEY	ANCHOR	DMC
□ Pale blue	975	3753
/ Green	208	563
● Dark pink	896	3721
‖ Medium pink	895	223

OUTLINES, WORKED IN BACK STITCH	
All outlines	Blue/grey (922, 930)

BOOKMARK CHART

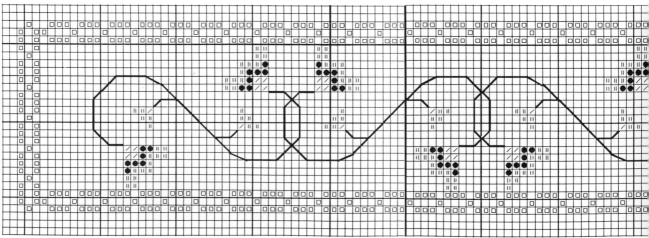

· NIGHT-DRESS · CASE ·

We continue the stylised floral theme in our monogrammed night-dress case. The cross stitch flowers here reflect those on the bookmark, but also have a similarity to the cushion motifs. With the addition of some broderie anglaise and satin ribbon, and the personalisation of the initials, you can add a touch of luxury to your bedroom.

Apart from the cross stitch design on the flap of this night-dress case, all the other sewing can be done by machine or by hand using cream cotton thread.

- *Stitch count: 102 x 70*
- *Design size: 7¹/₂ x 5in (19 x 12.5cm)*
- *32 x 14in (82 x 35.5cm) 14 count cream Aida fabric*
- *32 x 14in (82 x 35.5cm) cream coloured lining material (curtain lining is ideal)*
- *50in (127cm) broderie anglaise ribbon, 2in (5cm) wide*
- *39in (1m) satin ribbon, ¹/₂in (1.25cm) wide*
- *One press-stud*
- *One reel cream cotton thread*
- *One skein of each colour of Anchor or DMC stranded cotton (floss), as listed in the colour key*

1 Fold over 10in (25.5cm) across a short end of the Aida fabric. This will form the front flap of the night-dress case, and it is on this area that you should first stitch the cross stitch design.

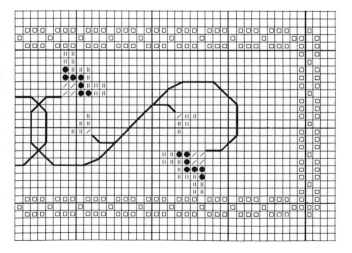

2 Choose the initials you require from the ornate alphabet on page 85 and draw these on to squared paper. Count how many squares they take up in height and width. Draw in a box around the initials leaving a gap of four squares all round the initials.
3 Using one strand of blue/grey stranded cotton (floss), back stitch this box on to the fabric first, leaving 5in (12.5cm) between the base of the box and the bottom edge of the fabric. See Fig 3.

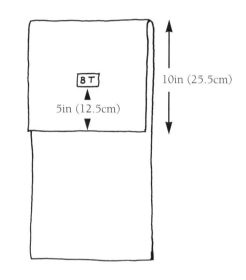

Fig 3 Start by stitching the box and initials

4 Following the chart on pages 60 and 61, and starting with your initials, work all the cross stitch using two strands of thread.
5 When you have completed all the cross stitching, use one strand of thread to work the back stitch.

MAKING UP
1 To complete the decoration of the flap cut two 14in (35.5cm) lengths of broderie anglaise ribbon and stitch these separately on to the edge of the Aida so that they overlap each other and just overlap the edge of the Aida by about ¹/₄in (5mm). See Fig 4 overleaf.
2 Cut 13in (33cm) of satin ribbon and stitch it to cover the top edge of the broderie anglaise ribbon. See Fig 5 overleaf. Stitch along both edges of the satin ribbon to hold it firmly in place. Don't worry about

the ends of the ribbon at this stage as they will be
hemmed in later.

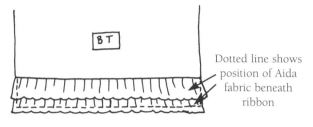

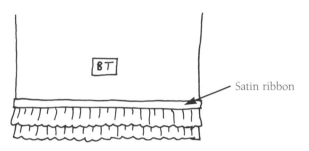

Fig 4 Stitch two overlapping layers of broderie anglaise ribbon
on to edge of fabric

Fig 5 Cover the edge of the broderie anglaise with satin ribbon
and stitch in place

3 Cut two 7in (18cm) pieces and one 11in (28cm)
piece of satin ribbon and pin these three pieces to
form the box around the cross stitch design (see
picture). Then stitch them in place. Now the flap
design is complete.

4 With right sides together, stitch the Aida and the
lining material together along three sides, leaving the
ribbon end unstitched. See Fig 6, page 61. Turn the
fabric right side out and press the side seams.

5 At the open end, unpick a few side seam stitches
sufficient to allow you to fold the raw edges of the
two fabrics inwards about $\frac{1}{2}$in (1.25cm), leaving the
broderie anglaise ribbon to overlap the two fabrics.
Pin together the turned in edges and either overstitch
or machine stitch them together to close up the open
end. Be careful not to catch the ribbon into this row
of stitching.

*The pretty night-dress case and bookmark make lovely additions
to any bedroom*

NIGHT-DRESS CASE CHART

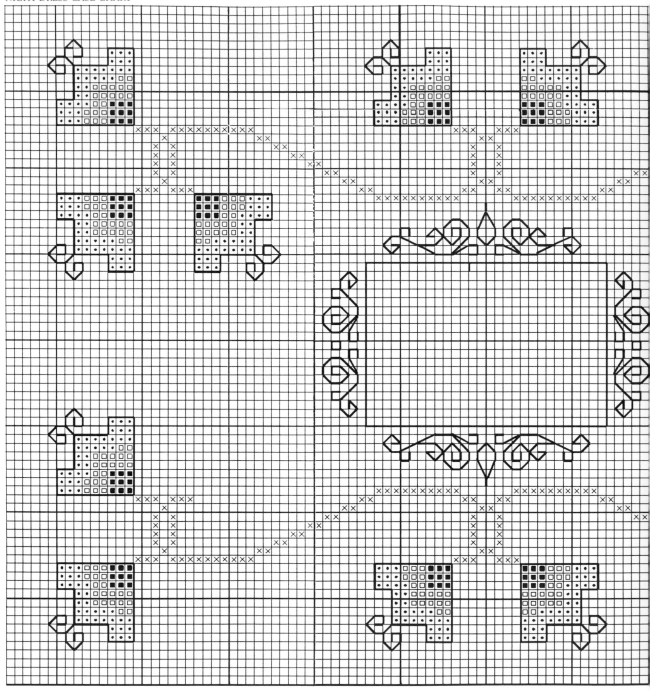

6 With the fabric stitching side down and the ribbon at the top, fold up a flap from the bottom of approximately 10in (25.5cm), forming an envelope. See Fig 7 opposite.

7 Cut two 11in (28cm) lengths of broderie anglaise ribbon and turn a ¼in (5mm) hem at each end of each piece.

Using one piece of broderie anglaise ribbon for each side seam, tuck the ribbon between the side edges, with the ribbon extending approximately 1in (2.5cm) above

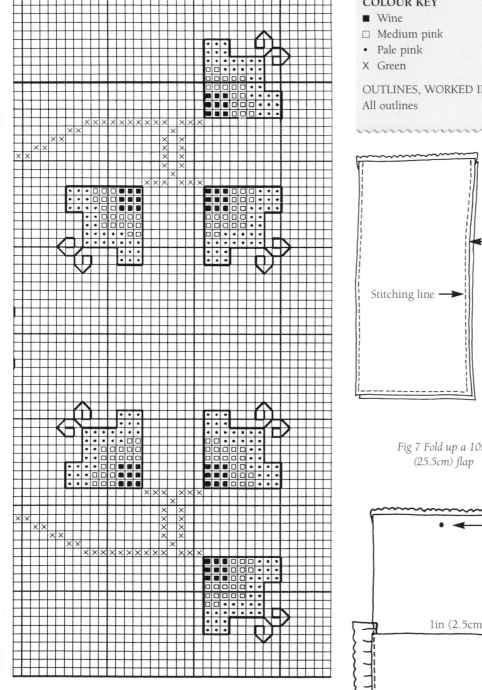

COLOUR KEY	ANCHOR	DMC
■ Wine	70	915
□ Medium pink	895	223
• Pale pink	48	963
X Green	208	563

OUTLINES, WORKED IN BACK STITCH
All outlines   Blue/grey (922, 930)

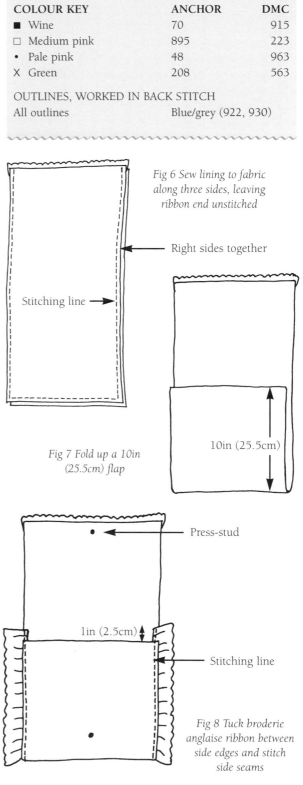

Fig 6 Sew lining to fabric along three sides, leaving ribbon end unstitched

Right sides together

Stitching line →

Fig 7 Fold up a 10in (25.5cm) flap

10in (25.5cm)

Press-stud

1in (2.5cm)

Stitching line

Fig 8 Tuck broderie anglaise ribbon between side edges and stitch side seams

the fold and pin the side edges together. See Fig 8 right.
8 Stitch up the side seams as close to the edge of the fabric as possible.
9 Fold the front flap down and sew on a press-stud to close the flap.

THE
·BATHROOM·
·Chapter Four·

It was only towards the end of Victoria's reign that fitted bathrooms with running water were drawn up in the plans for new houses. Before that, people washed at a wash-stand in the bedroom or dressing room, and water was brought in to fill the wash bowl. The first baths and wash-basins were plumbed into existing dressing rooms, which then became bathrooms. Later as bathrooms became the norm, styles in hygienic tiled decor began to flourish. So, the bathroom we portray here in our house may well be a refurbished dressing room off the master bedroom, but we have given it all the grandeur of a purpose-built late-Victorian masterpiece. The roll-top bath is free standing with elaborate brass feet. The wash-basin, shelves and shower plumbing are solid and glowing in ceramic, mahogany and brass.

· BATHROOM · PICTURE ·

Light pastel shades of blue and yellow echo the bright and airy look of the nursery, in contrast to the heavy formal look of the bedroom and drawing room. The use of alternate cross stitch in these pale shades helps to emphasise this effect of lightness.

We have often repeated patterns, taking advantage of the fact that they can be adapted and presented in a fresh context, whilst giving continuity of design. Here is an example, where the shell pattern on the edge of the blind is repeated successfully on both the bath and the edge of the wash-basin. You will find this shell motif again in our suggested towel edging on page 66. Notice also that the tiny Greek key pattern hinted at in outline on the towel in the bathroom scene appears again later in this chapter on page 66 where it has been enlarged and developed further to form another towel edging pattern.

- *Stitch count: 84 x 84*
- *Design size: 6 x 6in (15 x 15cm)*
- *10 x 10in (25.5 x 25.5cm) 14 count Aida fabric*
- *One skein of each colour of Anchor or DMC stranded cotton (floss) as listed in the colour key*

1 Before you start stitching, read through the preparation instructions on page 122 to find out how to mark the centre of your fabric.

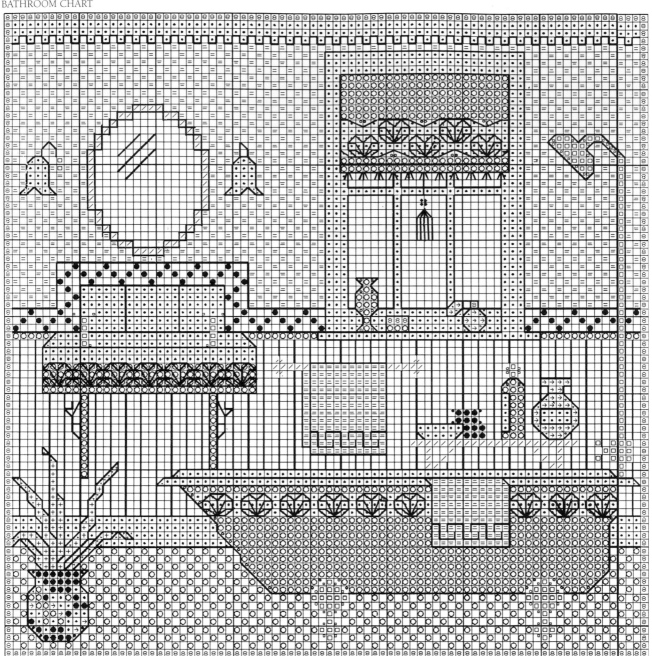

COLOUR KEY	ANCHOR	DMC
8 Blue/grey	922	930
• White	01	White
= Yellow	300	745
○ Palest blue	975	3753
/ Mahogany	351	400
■ Medium blue	137	798
→ Mauve	109	210
+ Pale green	208	563
□ Gold	Cristallina (use three strands)	

OUTLINES, WORKED IN BACK STITCH

Walls below dado	Palest blue (975, 3753)
Blind, bottles on shelf, tiles, shells on bath, lights, plant pot	Medium blue (137, 798)
Mirror frame	Mahogany (351, 400)
Light fittings (use three strands)	Gold (Cristallina)
Plant	Dark green (879, 500)
All other outlines	Blue/grey (922, 930)

2 Following the chart opposite, and starting either at the centre or if you prefer at the border, work all the cross stitch using two strands of thread except for the gold thread which requires three strands. See the stitch instructions on page 122.

3 When you have completed the cross stitching, use one strand of thread to work the back stitch.

MOUNTING AND FRAMING

If you intend to frame this design as an individual picture, read the hints on page 125 for help with mounting and framing.

If this picture is going to form part of the complete house, turn to page 110 for instructions on how to assemble the wall-hanging.

· TOWEL · BORDERS ·

 Towels can be embellished with cross stitch to great effect. See page 127 for suppliers details. Here we have enlarged two bathroom design motifs to add a classical touch to bathroom towels. Colours can be chosen to tone with your bathroom decor, or you may choose to use just one design but stitched in different colourways on each towel for personal identification.

Please note that the squares of our towel fabric are slightly rectangular, giving the design a 'drawn out' look compared with the chart.

- *Stitch count: width 51 squares*
- *Design size: width 2¹/₂in (6.5cm)*
- *One towel with an evenweave border*
- *One skein of each colour of Anchor or DMC stranded cotton (floss) as listed in the colour key*

1 As there is no beginning or end to these patterns, it does not matter whereabouts along either pattern you begin. Simply start at the centre of your evenweave border, and stitch the design from the centre in cross stitch using two strands of thread. See the stitch instructions on page 122.

2 Complete the design by working the border patterns using two strands of thread in the contrasting colour.

3 As the back is going to be visible when the towel is

in use, keep the back as tidy as possible, and cut off any ends of thread that still remain. If you sew a length of ribbon, the same width as the border, over the back, this will hide and protect the stitching.

GREEK KEY DESIGN

This design is reminiscent of Greek temples, Roman baths and spa hotels! In other words it is a classical design which has been revived time and time again. Needless to say, the Victorians claimed it and used it widely as a decorative edging for tiles and anaglyptas.

GREEK KEY CHART ON PAGES 66–67

COLOUR KEY		ANCHOR	DMC
●	Pink	48	963
□	Green	185	964

SHELL DESIGN

Here we have enlarged the shell motif from the bathroom scene and alternated it with a type of fleur-de-lys pattern in traditional shades of blue.

SHELL CHART ON PAGES 66–67

COLOUR KEY		ANCHOR	DMC
□	Palest blue	975	3753
○	Light blue	130	799
■	Medium blue	137	798

GREEK KEY CHART

SHELL CHART

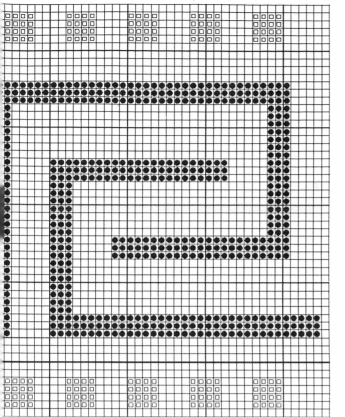

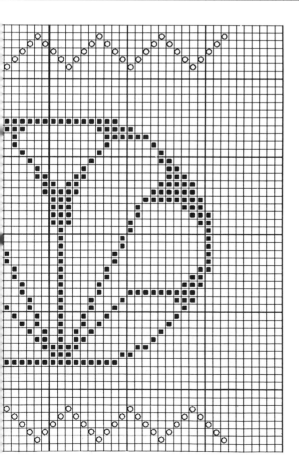

• CLEANLINESS • IS •
• NEXT • TO • GODLINESS •

 Here is a very well-known saying given a light-hearted slant to bring it into modern times. You will recognise the classical border from our towel design, which once again mimics the grand tile borders of bygone times.

- *Stitch count: 88 x 75*
- *Design size: 6¹/₂ x 5¹/₂in (16.5 x 14cm)*
- *10 x 9in (25.5 x 23cm) 14 count Aida fabric*
- *One skein of each colour of Anchor or DMC stranded cotton (floss) as listed in the colour key*

1 Before you start stitching, read through the preparation instructions on page 122, to find out how to mark the centre of your fabric.
2 Following the chart on page 71, and starting at the top centre of the border, work all the cross stitch of the border using two strands of turquoise thread. See the stitch instructions on page 122.
3 Using two strands of pink thread, work the rest of the border in back stitch.
4 Using two strands of thread, work the rest of the cross stitch, except for shower fitting and bath feet.
5 Use three strands of gold thread for both cross stitch and back stitch in the shower fitting and also for the cross stitch of the bath feet.
6 When you have completed the cross stitching, use two strands of blue/grey thread to work the words in back stitch. Also, use two strands of mahogany thread to work the backbrush in back stitch.

These simple border patterns, the classical Greek key and traditional shell, can be worked in any colour to match the decor of your own bathroom

7 Finally, using one strand of thread, work the rest of the back stitch.

MOUNTING AND FRAMING
Read the hints on page 125 for help with mounting and framing. If you can, choose a frame with an antique look which also suits the decor of your own bathroom. Something with a mottled marble effect, reminiscent of old-fashioned Turkish baths or spa hotels of the Victoria era, would be ideal.

CLEANLINESS IS NEXT TO GODLINESS CHART ON PAGE 71

COLOUR KEY	ANCHOR	DMC
X Turquoise	185	964
● Light blue	130	799
/ Peach	4146	3774
• White	01	White
■ Pink	895	223
△ Gold	Cristallina (use three strands)	

OUTLINES, WORKED IN BACK STITCH

Writing (two strands)	Blue/grey (922, 930)
Backbrush (two strands)	Mahogany (351, 400)
Border (two strands)	Pink (895, 223)
Shower fitting (three strands)	Gold (Cristallina)
Flower pattern on bath, water (one strand)	Turquoise (185, 964)
All other outlines (one strand)	Blue/grey (922, 930)

This well-known saying adds a delightful touch to the Victorian-style bathroom

CLEANLINESS IS NEXT TO GODLINESS CHART

THE
·NURSERY·
· Chapter Five ·

Nurseries usually occupied the attic space where windows were high, therefore out of reach of small children, where toys or even swings could be hung from the exposed rafters, and where light and air could circulate. In larger houses there would also have been an adjacent room for the nanny, whose status being higher than that of cook or gardener, entitled her to some privacy. The children's nursery in our Victorian house illustrates the same furnishing principles as would happily be used today: bright cheerful colours, with hard wearing, washable surfaces.

· NURSERY · PICTURE ·

Our nursery bedspreads cleverly imitate Log Cabin patchwork design, an early import from American colonial style. It is remarkable how many styles can be effectively represented in cross stitch. Throughout our book we have experimented with the abundance of patterns which were appropriated by the Victorians from around the globe in the days of Empire. Much of the nursery scene seems very familiar, and similar to a modern child's bedroom. But there are subtle differences. For example, the toys must be stitched to look more square and solid than their modern day counterparts, being made

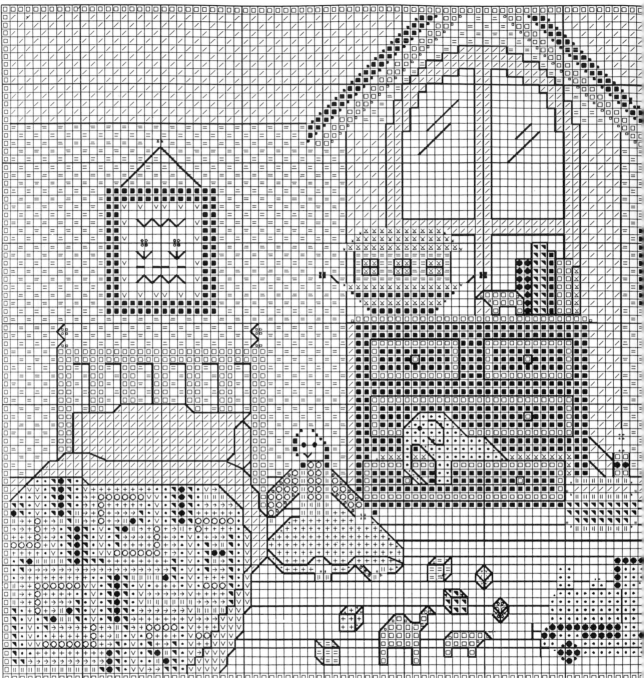

of wood and simply painted, or in the case of soft-toys being firmly stuffed and constructed of made-to-last calicos and cottons. Teddy peeping out of bed and the little be-ribboned hat swinging from the bed-post give this room the personal touches that bring the picture to life. We always suggest including personal touches in our room scenes; why not stitch in something personal to you or your family and transform the design into your very own unique picture?

If you intend to stitch the nursery design as a part of the whole house, and not as an individual picture, do not stitch it on a separate piece of fabric from the roof. Instead, turn to page 110 and follow the instructions for stitching the roof and the top of the house before stitching the nursery.

COLOUR KEY	ANCHOR	DMC
□ Light brown	373	437
/ White	01	White
X Grey	400	317
‖ Wine	70	915
○ Light pink	48	963
+ Medium pink	895	223
→ Dark pink	896	3721
V Palest blue	975	3753
• Light blue	130	799
■ Medium blue	137	798
● Dark blue	149	336
= Yellow	300	745
■ Mahogany	351	400

OUTLINES, WORKED IN BACK STITCH

Ark windows, drum	White (01, White)
Picture frames, floor, doll's hair, front and back of ark (see illustration), doll's face	Mahogany (351, 400)
Elephant, flowers on small picture, train	Dark blue (149, 336)
Doll's clothes	Wine (70, 915)
Samplers (see illustration)	Light blue (130, 799)
Sampler (see illustration)	Medium pink (895, 223)
All other outlines	Grey (400, 317)

FRENCH KNOTS

Eyes of teddy bear and elephant	Grey (400, 317)
Eyes of doll	Mahogany (351, 400)

2 Following the chart above, and starting either at the centre or if you prefer at the border, work all the cross stitch using two strands of thread. See the stitch instructions on page 122.

3 When you have completed the cross stitching, use one strand of thread to work the backstitch.

4 Finally, using one strand of thread work the eyes of the doll, teddy and elephant in French knots following the stitch instructions on page 124.

MOUNTING AND FRAMING

If you intend to frame this design as an individual picture, read the hints on page 125 for help with mounting and framing. If you have stitched the nursery as part of the top of the house, turn to page 110 for instructions on how to assemble the wall-hanging.

- Stitch count: 120 x 84
- Design size: 9 x 7in (23 x 18cm)
- 14 x 12in (35.5 x 30cm) 14 count Aida fabric
- One skein of each colour of Anchor or DMC stranded cotton (floss) as listed in the colour key

1 Before you start stitching, read through the preparation instructions on page 122 to find out how to mark the centre of your fabric.

· VICTORIAN · TOYS ·

The toys in the following four pictures are, like the toys in our nursery, based on the authentic shapes, colours and textures of the time. These pictures show how beautifully simple yet solid heavy mahogany frames can look, even on such small pictures without mounts.

COLOUR KEY	ANCHOR	DMC
■ Dark brown	381	838
• Light brown	373	437
□ Maroon	22	814
/ Peach	9575	353
X Grey	399	415
V White	01	White
● Dark blue	149	336

OUTLINES, WORKED IN BACK STITCH
Beefeater tunic decoration
  (not body outline) — Light brown (373, 437)
Train — Maroon (22, 814)
All other outlines — Dark brown (381, 838)

FRENCH KNOTS
Eyes and nose of teddy bear — Dark brown (381, 838)

ROCKING HORSE

- *Stitch count: 70 x 50*
- *Design size: 5 x 3¹/₂in (12.5 x 9cm)*
- *9 x 8in (23 x 20cm) 14 count Aida fabric*
- *One skein of each colour of Anchor or DMC stranded cotton (floss) as listed in the colour key*

1 Before you start stitching, read through the preparation instructions on page 122, to find out how to mark the centre of your fabric.

2 Following the chart below, and starting at the centre, work all the cross stitch using two strands of thread. See the stitch instructions on page 122.

3 When you have completed the cross stitching, use one strand of thread to work the back stitch.

4 Finally, using one strand of thread, work French knots for the eyes and nose of the teddy bear, following the stitch instructions on page 124.

ROCKING HORSE CHART

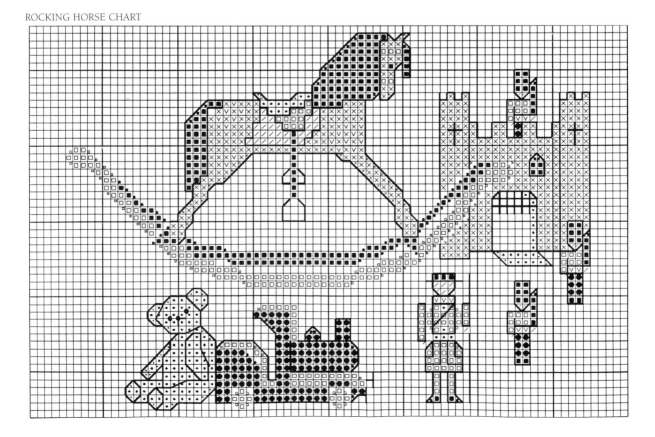

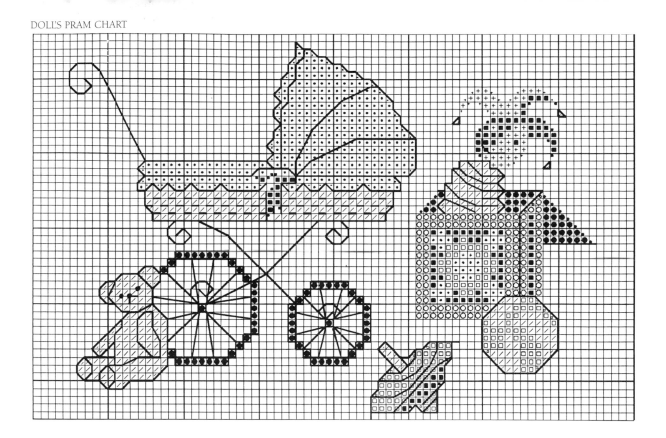

MOUNTING AND FRAMING

Read the hints on page 125 for help with mounting and framing. Notice that we have chosen oval frames for all the Victorian toys designs. Although these frames are made of re-constituted wood, and as such are not very expensive, they are a good imitation of solid wood. Most high street framers have good quality inexpensive frames which look stylistically 'Victorian'. An alternative would be to use rectangular mounts with an oval aperture which would fit into standard rectangular frames.

DOLL'S PRAM

- *Stitch count: 70 x 50*
- *Design size: 5 x 3¹/₂in (12.5 x 9cm)*
- *9 x 8in (23 x 20cm) 14 count Aida fabric*
- *One skein of each colour of Anchor or DMC stranded cotton (floss) as listed in the colour key*

1 Before you start stitching, read through the preparation instructions on page 122, to find out how to mark the centre of your fabric.
2 Following the chart above, and starting at the centre, work all the cross stitch using two strands of thread. See the stitch instructions on page 122.
3 When you have completed the cross stitching, use one strand of thread to work the back stitch.

COLOUR KEY	ANCHOR	DMC
● Dark brown	381	838
/ Light brown	373	437
■ Maroon	22	814
• Peach	9575	353
□ Blue/grey	922	930
○ Green	879	500
+ Gold	307	783

OUTLINES, WORKED IN BACK STITCH
Spinning top, pram canopy
  and cover   Maroon (22, 814)
Ball   Blue/grey (922, 930)
All other outlines   Dark brown (381, 838)

FRENCH KNOTS
Eyes and nose of teddy bear   Dark brown (381, 838)

4 Finally, using one strand of thread, work French knots for the eyes and nose of the teddy bear following the stitch instructions on page 124.

Overleaf These pictures of traditional children's toys look particularly charming grouped in matching frames

MOUNTING AND FRAMING
Follow the instructions for Rocking Horse on page 78.

DOLL'S HOUSE
- *Stitch count: 70 x 50*
- *Design size: 5 x 3¹/₂in (12.5 x 9cm)*
- *9 x 8in (23 x 20cm) 14 count Aida fabric*
- *One skein of each colour of Anchor or DMC stranded cotton (floss) as listed in the colour key*

1 Before you start stitching, read through the preparation instructions on page 122, to find out how to mark the centre of your fabric.
2 Following the chart above, and starting at the centre, work all the cross stitch using two strands of thread. See the stitch instructions on page 122.
3 When you have completed the cross stitching, use one strand of thread to work the back stitch.
4 Finally, using one strand of thread, work French knots for the eyes and nose of the teddy bear and the eyes of the doll following the stitch instructions on page 124.

MOUNTING AND FRAMING
Follow the instructions for Rocking Horse on page 78.

COLOUR KEY		ANCHOR	DMC
●	Dark brown	381	838
V	Light brown	373	437
X	Maroon	22	814
•	Peach	9575	353
=	Blue/grey	922	930
□	Off-white	830	3033
\	Gold	307	783
■	Green	879	500

OUTLINES, WORKED IN BACK STITCH
Drum	Off-white (830, 3033)
Windows	Blue/grey (922, 930)
All other outlines	Dark brown (381, 838)

FRENCH KNOTS
Eyes and nose of teddy bear, eyes of doll	Dark brown (381, 838)

NOAH'S ARK
- *Stitch count: 70 x 50*
- *Design size: 5 x 3¹/₂in (12.5 x 9cm)*
- *9 x 8in (23 x 20cm) 14 count Aida fabric*
- *One skein of each colour of Anchor or DMC stranded cotton (floss) as listed in the colour key*

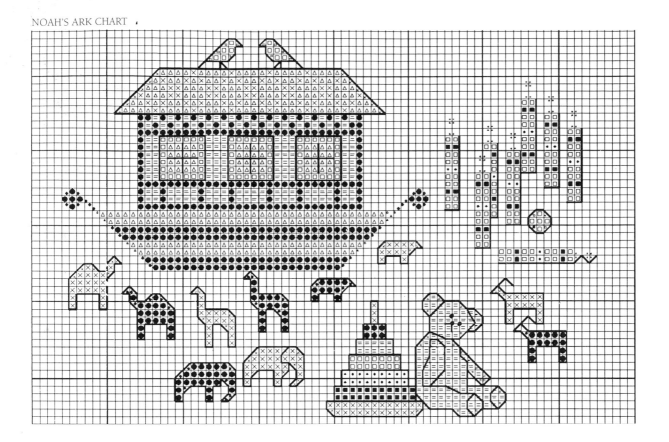

COLOUR KEY	ANCHOR	DMC
● Dark brown	351	400
X Light brown	373	437
△ Grey	400	317
= Yellow	300	745
□ White	01	White
• Pink	895	223
■ Blue	149	336

OUTLINES, WORKED IN BACK STITCH
Window bars	White (01, white)
Teddy bear, animals	Dark brown (351, 400)
All other outlines	Grey (400, 317)

FRENCH KNOTS
Eyes and nose of teddy bear	Dark brown (381, 838)

knots for the eyes and nose of the teddy bear following the stitch instructions on page 124.

MOUNTING AND FRAMING
Follow the instructions for Rocking Horse on page 78.

PERSONALISING A DESIGN

In this chapter we include some varied alphabets and ideas for personalising any of the designs in this book. The two name plates on page 83, suitable for a child's bedroom door, use the back stitch alphabet from page 82. The Victorian toy designs lend themselves to this type of use, as well as being suitable for birth samplers or birthday presents.

The more elaborate alphabet on page 85 can be used in the same way, or you can use a mixture of two alphabets, making just the initial letters elaborate. Some of these ideas are illustrated on page 84.

Always draw your name, initials or date of birth on to squared paper before you attempt to stitch it. In this way you can count the squares and make sure that you centre it correctly.

1 Before you start stitching, read through the preparation instructions on page 122, to find out how to mark the centre of your fabric.
2 Following the chart above, and starting at the centre, work all the cross stitch using two strands of thread. See the stitch instructions on page 122.
3 When you have completed the cross stitching, use one strand of thread to work the back stitch.
4 Finally, using one strand of thread, work French

Opposite *The addition of a name makes a personalised picture for a child's bedroom*

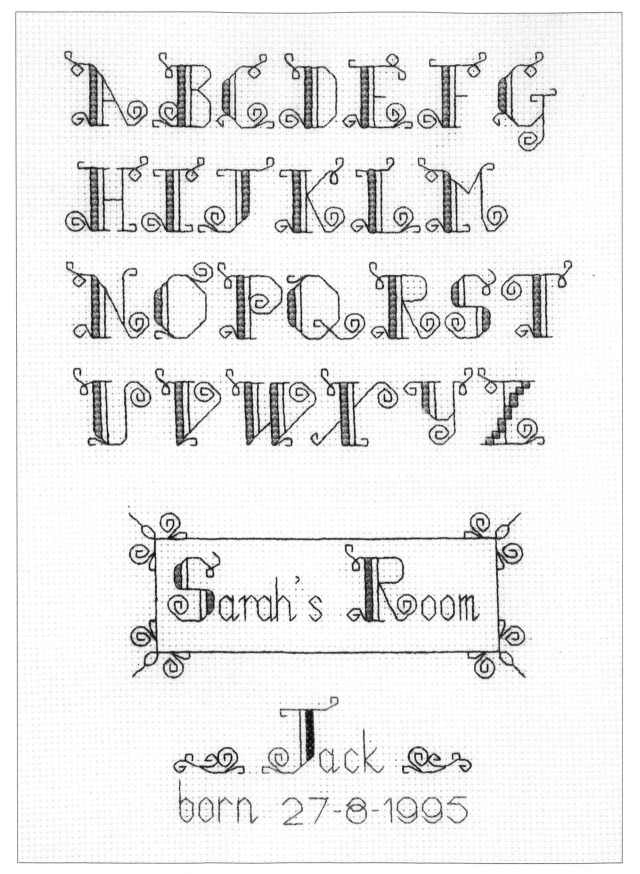

· SOME · ONE · CAME · KNOCKING ·

When we were young, children learned poems at school. The poems were often, as this example is, Victorian. There is mystery and melodrama, danger and security in this Walter De La Mare classic. This is an opportunity to use a simple but elegant alphabet style for the script and use symbols of the mystery of night; a moon and the trailing branches of an overgrown tree to illustrate the theme. Books and toys and teddy at the bottom of the picture return us safely home!

- *Stitch count: 163 x 124*
- *Design size: 12 x 9in (30 x 23cm)*
- *17 x 14in (43 x 35.5cm) 14 count Aida fabric*
- *One skein of each colour of Anchor or DMC stranded cotton (floss) as listed in the colour key*

1 Before you start stitching, read through the preparation instructions on page 122 to find out how to mark the centre of your fabric.
2 Following the chart on pages 88 and 89, and starting at the border, work all the cross stitch using two strands of thread. See the stitch instructions on page 122.
3 When you have completed the cross stitching, use two strands of thread to work the words of the poem in back stitch.
4 Using one strand of thread, work the remaining outlining in back stitch.

5 Finally, using one strand of thread work the eyes and nose of the teddy bear in French knots following the stitch instructions on page 124.

MOUNTING AND FRAMING
Read the hints on page 125 for help with mounting and framing. You could choose an antique-look frame to add to the childhood nostalgia of this poem.

CHART ON PAGES 88–89

COLOUR KEY		ANCHOR	DMC
□	Blue/grey	922	930
△	Olive green	846	936
X	Grey/green	876	502
●	Dark green	879	500
=	Yellow	300	745
•	Stone	393	640
/	Dark brown	381	838
■	Maroon	22	814

OUTLINES, WORKED IN BACK STITCH

Poem (use two strands), poet's name (use one strand)	Dark blue (149, 336)
Maroon book top	Maroon (22, 814)
Dark green books	Dark green (879, 500)
Grey/green book	Grey/green (876, 502)
Moon	Stone (393, 640)
All other outlines	Dark brown (381, 838)

FRENCH KNOTS

Eyes and nose of teddy bear	Dark brown (381, 838)

Some one came knocking
At my wee small door;
Some one came knocking
I'm sure—sure—sure;
I listened, I opened,
I looked to left and right,
But nought there was a-stirring
In the still dark night;

WALTER DE LA MARE

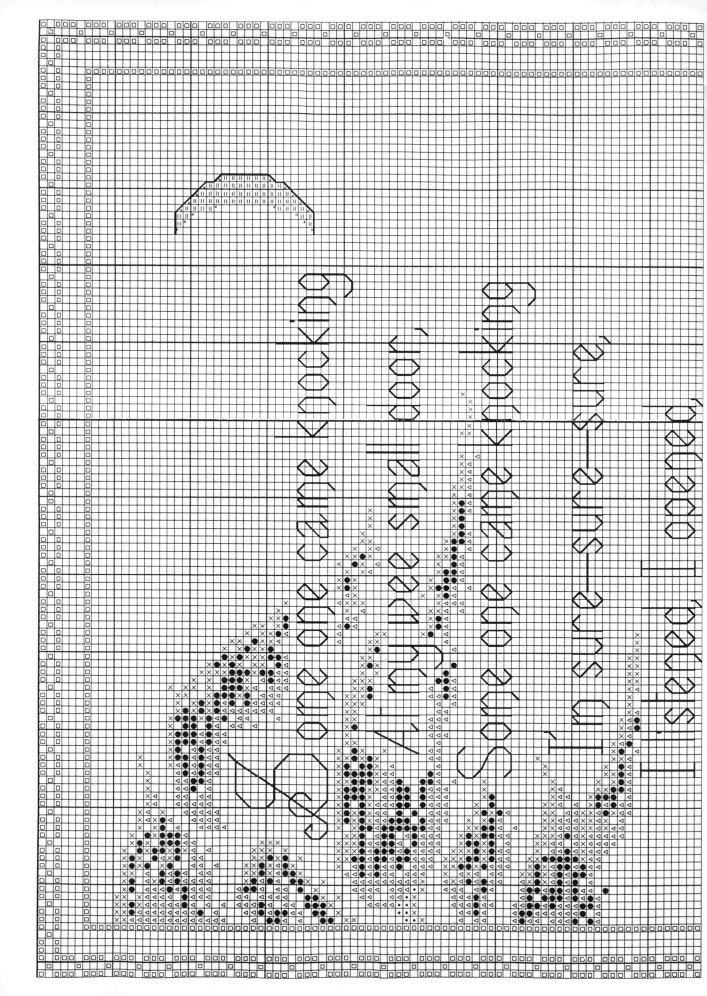

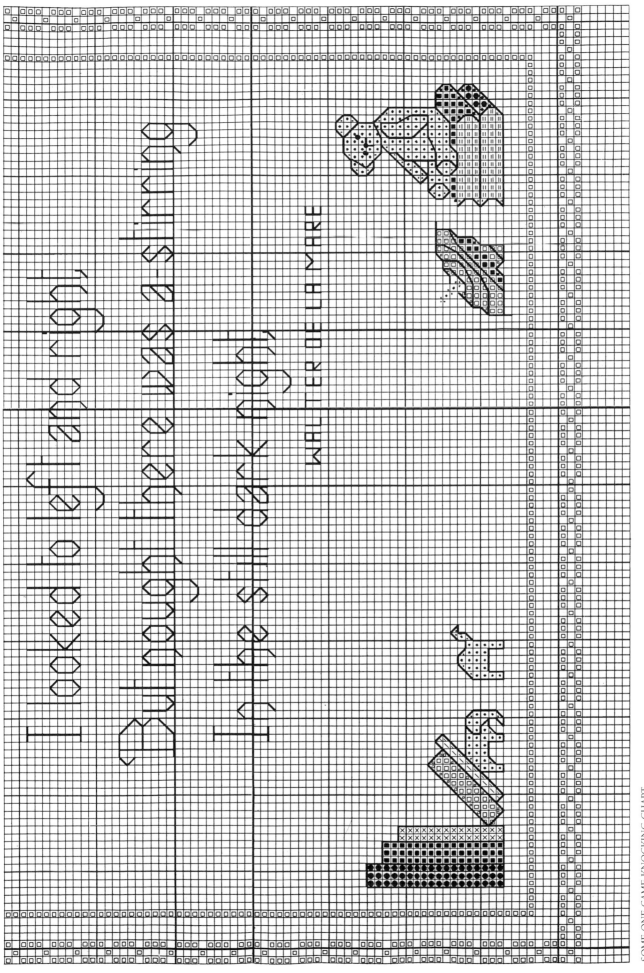

'I looked to left and right,

But nought there was a-stirring

In the still dark night;

WALTER DE LA MARE

SOME ONE CAME KNOCKING CHART

·ENTRANCE· HALL·AND·STAIRS·

· Chapter Six ·

The Victorian hall had to bridge the gap between the often gloomy world outside and the sumptuous interior. It had to be functional in keeping the weather out as well as being decorously inviting. The door itself was recognised as the focal point, offering to the visitor that all-so-important first impression of the owner's social standing. Early architectural style favoured the security of a solid mahogany or oak front door which made the hall-way very dark. So it became fashionable for a rectangular or semi-circular fanlight to be incorporated above the door to allow natural light to enter. By the turn of the century the lighter, more ornate stained glass panels had been introduced, both in the door itself, and also in side panels flanking the door.

· FRONT · DOOR · PICTURE ·

We can all recognise a Victorian entrance and front door, despite being aware that the designers of the time took every style in history and made it their own. Our entrance reflects several of these styles. The portico follows the Italianate influence of the 1850s, in keeping with the rest of the exterior. But instead of building in a plain wooden door, we have leapt forward in time to include the more ornate stained glass panels which are typical of the late Victorian or Edwardian period.

The walls and probably the columns would have been stucco rather than stone, and this is easily represented in alternate cross stitch on the rear wall and in close cross stitch on the columns, with back stitch in dark grey for the elaborate scrolling and the stepping at the head and foot of the pillars.

The door should be filled in with cross stitch then worked over in back stitch using black thread to mark the panel outlines. Stained glass is best worked, as here, in a limited number of pale colours on a pale background to give an impression of the diffusion of light. The individual colours are brought into focus by the dark grey outlining which mimics the lead.

The roof slates are worked in a traditional blue/grey, and this is balanced by the pretty tile pattern below on the step. Here the regular tessellating shapes, achieved with diagonal half stitches, give an elegant Italianate signature.

COLOUR KEY	ANCHOR	DMC				
< Off-white	830	3033	+ Dark grey	400	317
/ Blue/grey	922	930	○ Light grey	399	415
‖ White	01	White	■ Mahogany	351	400
			△ Green	208	563

X Yellow	300	745
● Wine	70	915
□ Pink	895	223
• Palest blue	975	3753

OUTLINES, WORKED IN BACK STITCH

Door (excluding stained glass), knocker, handle, letterbox	Black (403, 310)
All other outlines	Dark grey (400, 317)

- *Stitch count: 147 x 78*
- *Design size: 11 x 6in (28 x 15cm)*
- *15 x 10in (38 x 25.5cm) 14 count Aida fabric*
- *Two skeins each of white, off-white and mahogany stranded cotton (floss)*
- *One skein of each of the other colours of stranded cotton (floss) as listed in the colour key*

1 Before you start stitching, read through the preparation instructions on page 122 to find out how to mark the centre of your fabric.

2 Following the chart on pages 92 and 93, and starting at the centre, work all the cross stitch using two strands of thread. See the stitch instructions on page 122.

3 Use one strand of thread to work the back stitch.

MOUNTING AND FRAMING

If you intend to frame this design as an individual picture, read the hints on page 125 for help with mounting and framing. If this picture is going to form part of the complete house, turn to page 110 for instructions on how to assemble the wall-hanging.

· THE · MAID ·

Framed by a pathway of lavender and the wrought iron gates to the walled garden, our maid is bringing into the house a basket of home-grown vegetables. She is formally dressed with starched white apron, cap, collar and cuffs. Full-time domestic help were often employed even when the house was not large enough for staff to live-in.

Realistic figures are a challenge in cross stitch; the tradition has been to make figures squared and cartoon like. We have tried to give our maid some seriousness and reality by gently curving and shaping her image and we think she fits well her elegant surroundings.

- *Stitch count: 90 x 50*
- *Design size: 7 x 4in (18 x 10cm)*
- *11 x 8in (28 x 20cm) 14 count Aida fabric*
- *One skein of each colour of Anchor or DMC stranded cotton (floss) as listed in the colour key*

1 Before you start stitching, read through the preparation instructions on page 122 to find out how to mark the centre of your fabric.

2 Following the chart on page 96, and starting either at the centre or if you prefer at the border, work all the cross stitch using two strands of thread. See the stitch instructions on page 122.

CHART ON PAGE 96

COLOUR KEY		ANCHOR	DMC
●	Blue/grey	922	930
‖	Off-white	830	3033
■	Lavender	109	210
△	Grey/green	876	502
■	Dark green	879	500
X	Grey	399	415
+	Stone	393	640
↑	Light yellowish brown	373	437
□	Dark brown	381	838
/	Pale peach	4146	3774
V	Dark peach	337	758
•	White	01	White

OUTLINES, WORKED IN BACK STITCH

Apron, blouse, cap	Blue/grey (922, 930)
Basket, skirt, shoes, hair, hands, carrots	Dark brown (381, 838)
Cabbage	Dark green (879, 500)
Carrot leaves, lavender	Grey/green (876, 502)
Gate, face, mouth	Grey (399, 415)
All other outlines	Stone (393, 640)

FRENCH KNOTS

Eyes	Grey (399, 415)

3 When you have completed the cross stitching, use one strand of thread to work the back stitch.

THE MAID CHART

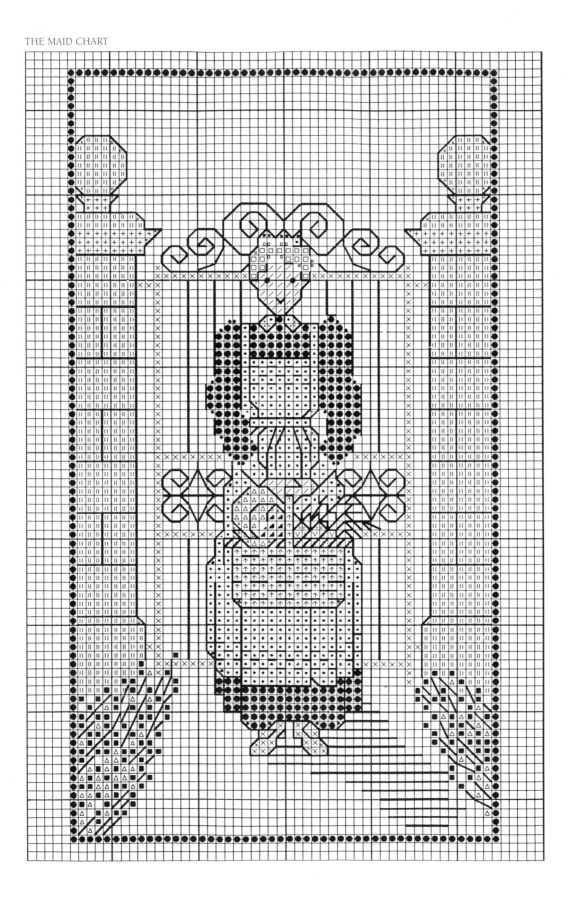

4 Finally, using one strand of thread, work French knots for the eyes where indicated on the chart following the stitch instructions on page 124.

MOUNTING AND FRAMING
Read the hints on page 125 for help with mounting and framing.

· PIN · CUSHION ·

The floors of porch, vestibule and hall, and sometimes even the front approach path, were both decorated and protected by hardwearing, easily cleaned tiles. The higher the status of the home, the more elaborately coloured and intricately patterned these tiles became. The tessellating patterns of the tiles reflected a renewed interest in medieval design, and in the planning stage, the designs were no doubt drawn out on squared paper, much like our cross stitch patterns today. Because of the perspective, it is very difficult to represent tiled floors in our room settings, but it is simplicity itself to copy a tile pattern in two dimensions and use it to decorate any object we choose. So here we have a pin cushion with authentic tile pattern design, stitched in the colours much loved by the Victorians.

- *Stitch count: 70 x 70*
- *Design size: 5 x 5in (12.5 x 12.5cm)*
- *6 x 6in (15 x 15cm) 14 count Aida fabric*
- *One skein of each colour of Anchor or DMC stranded cotton (floss) as listed in the colour key*
- *6 x 6in (15 x 15cm) backing fabric. Practically any fabric will do for the backing. We chose cream coloured cotton with a small terracotta motif to tone with the tile shades in the cross stitch design*
- *Wadding (batting) or any suitable stuffing such as old cut-up tights (panty hose)*

1 Before you start stitching, read through the preparation instructions on page 122 to find out how to mark the centre of your fabric.
2 Following the chart on page 98, and starting either at the centre or if you prefer at the border, work all the cross stitch using two strands of thread. See the stitch instructions on page 122.

MAKING UP
1 When you have completed the cross stitch, cut your fabric down to leave ½in (1.25cm) border around the design, and cut your backing material to exactly the same size.
2 With right sides together, pin then machine or hand stitch the two fabrics together, sewing as closely as possible to the cross stitch border, and leaving a 2in (5cm) gap in the fourth side. See Fig 9.

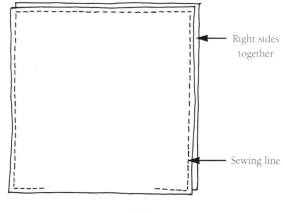

Right sides
together

Sewing line

Fig 9

3 Turn the fabrics right side out and stuff the pin cushion with wadding (batting) or other suitable material. Take great care to push the wadding (batting) tightly into the corners and add enough to make a very firm pin cushion.
4 Finally, turn in the remaining raw edges and over-stitch them together by hand.

PIN CUSHION CHART

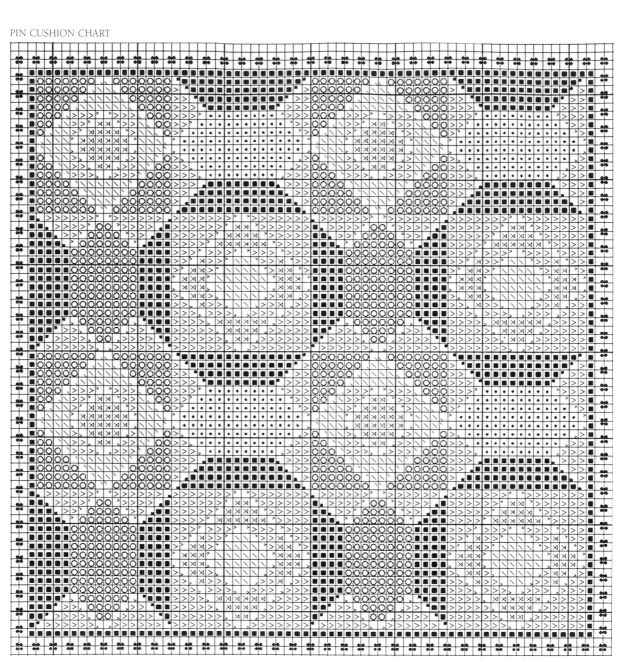

COLOUR KEY	ANCHOR	DMC
■ Dark brown	381	838
• Sandstone	373	437
> Terracotta	5975	356
⋈ White	01	White
\ Blue	137	798
○ Yellow	300	745
● Blue/grey	922	930

• PERFUMED • SACHET •

 Like our pin cushion, this design is based on an actual Victorian hall tile pattern but in this version the colours are less traditional.

❧

- *Stitch count: 36 x 36*
- *Design size: 2¹/₂ x 2¹/₂in (6.5 x 6.5cm)*
- *3¹/₂ x 3¹/₂in (9 x 9cm) 14 count Aida fabric*
- *One skein of each colour of Anchor or DMC stranded cotton (floss) as listed in the colour key*
- *3¹/₂ x 3¹/₂in (9 x 9cm) backing fabric – see pin cushion for details*

- *13in (33cm) cream coloured gathered lace approximately 1in (2.5cm) wide*
- *3in (7.5cm) cream coloured ribbon approximately ¹/₂in (1.25cm) wide*
- *Wadding (batting) see pin cushion for details*
- *A few drops of perfume oil – the kind used in pot pourri*

1 Before you start stitching, read through the preparation instructions on page 122 to find out how to mark the centre of your fabric.

2 Following the chart on page 99, and starting either at the centre or if you prefer at the border, work all the cross stitch using two strands of thread. See the stitch instructions on page 122.

PERFUMED SACHET CHART

COLOUR KEY	ANCHOR	DMC
● Dark brown	381	838
\ Terracotta	5975	356
• Yellow	300	745
□ Maroon	22	814
⋈ Blue	137	798

MAKING UP

1 When you have completed the cross stitch design, cut the fabric down to leave a ½in (1.25cm) border around the stitching, and cut the backing material to exactly the same size.

2 Tack (baste) the gathered lace to the right side of the Aida fabric around the cross stitching, with the frill of the lace facing inwards towards the centre of the design. See Fig 10.

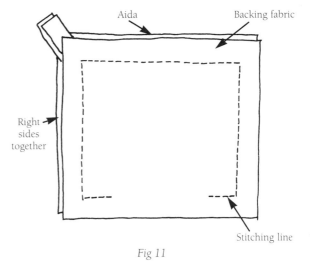

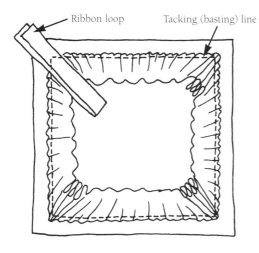

Fig 10

3 Tack (baste) a loop of ribbon to one corner of the design, with the loop pointing inwards towards the centre of the design. See Fig 10.

4 Place the piece of backing material, right side down, on to the lace, and match the side edges of the backing to the side edges of the Aida.

5 Machine or hand sew around the edges leaving part of the fourth side open, as shown in Fig 11. Sew as closely as possible to the cross stitch border ensuring that you catch in the edge of the lace.

Fig 11

6 Turn the sachet right side out so that the lace frill and the ribbon loop are now around the outside edge.

7 Sprinkle a few drops of perfume oil on to some wadding (batting) or other suitable material and use this to stuff the sachet.

8 Turn in the remaining raw edges and over-sew them together by hand. See Fig 12.

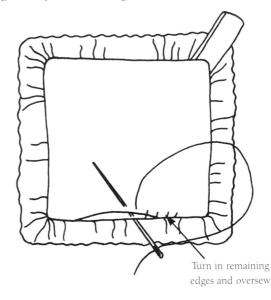

Fig 12 Sachet seen from back

Opposite The perfumed sachet (left) and the pincushion (right) are inspired by the patterns often found in the tiled floors of Victorian hallways

· STAIRS · AND · LANDING ·

Linking together the different rooms of the house, which differed widely in their styles and functions, the hall, stairs, landings and corridors gave less scope for dense decoration. However, these areas were by no means plain. The stairs were generally made of wood and were often elaborately decorated, with a mahogany handrail, turned balusters and carved newel posts.

We have chosen colours in our genteel hall which are a bridge between the darker shades of the formal rooms and the light and airy tones of the practical family areas of bathroom, nursery and kitchen.

As with the heavy fringing of the drawing room curtains, we have used more back stitch than is normal in our hall curtains to achieve the impression of luxurious texture. It takes a little practise to perfect this stitching technique but it is well worth the effort.

You will recognise the design of the stained glass window at the turn of the stair as it matches the panels in the front door. However, in this image, the light is coming into the house from outside, so the look of the glass must be lighter and brighter. Repeats of patterns in this way give harmony to the whole project.

Carpet, wallpaper and tiles provided copious opportunities for patterns. And the wall space, especially in stairwells, was perfect for an array of pictures. One particularly favoured decorative feature was the dado, which had to be hard-wearing and washable as well as attractive. Marbled paper was used at first, but this was later replaced by leather-paper or embossed anaglypta.

Varied use of cross stitch and back stitch give the impression of anaglypta on the dado, and of panelling under the balustrade. Obvious shading differences indicate the effect of light on the treads and risers of the carpet on the steps.

Each of the other room designs that make up our Victorian house can be stitched and framed to make individual pictures without any modification. The stairs and landing can also be stitched as an individual picture by omitting the lower stairs and continuing the border across the bottom of the picture. The design then measures 120 squares by 84 squares. It is illustrated opposite with the stairs included.

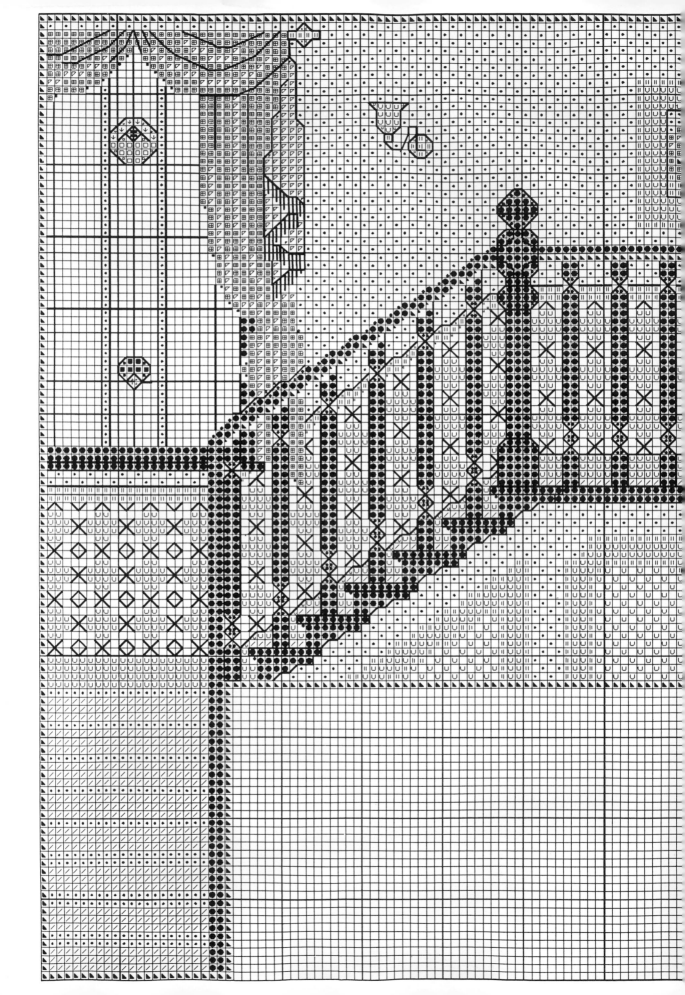

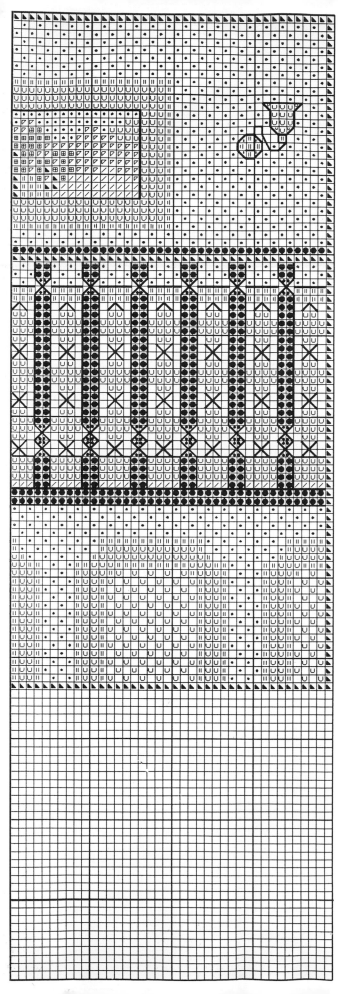

COLOUR KEY	ANCHOR	DMC
● Mahogany	351	400
◣ Dark brown	381	838
U Off-white	830	3033
‖ Light brown	373	437
• Palest blue	975	3753
⊞ Dark green	879	500
▽ Pale green	208	563
↓ Yellow	300	745
■ Wine	70	915
☐ Pink	895	223
/ Blue/grey	922	930

OUTLINES, WORKED IN BACK STITCH

Curtain pole	Dark brown (381, 838)
Curtain fringe	Dark green (879, 500)
Window, dado rail, lights, picture	Blue/grey (922, 930)
Wallpaper, skirting board	Light brown (373, 437)
All other outlines	Black (403, 310)

- *Stitch count: 120 x 120*
- *Design size: 9 x 9in (23 x 23cm)*
- *13 x 13in (33 x 33cm) 14 count Aida fabric*
- *One skein of each colour of Anchor or DMC stranded cotton (floss) as listed in the colour key*

1 Before you start stitching, read through the preparation instructions on page 122 to find out how to mark the centre of your fabric.

2 Following the chart opposite, and starting either at the centre or if you prefer at the border, work all the cross stitch using two strands of thread.

3 When you have completed the cross stitching, use one strand of thread to work the back stitch.

MOUNTING AND FRAMING

If you intend to frame this design as an individual picture, read the hints on page 125 for help with mounting and framing. If this picture is going to form part of the complete house, turn to page 110 for instructions on how to assemble the wall-hanging.

STAIRS AND LANDING CHART

· HOME · IS · WHERE ·
· THE · HEART · IS ·

 This well-known saying expresses the kind of sentiment often embroidered and framed to adorn the hall of a nineteenth-century home. In true Victorian fashion we have taken the style of a previous era, a Jacobean flower design, and translated this into cross stitch. You will recognise the traditional Jacobean motifs of rose, daisy, acorn and oak leaf, as well as the more fantastical flower designs beloved of the genre. The fine detail is achieved with the abundant use of diagonal half cross stitches and plenty of back stitch for flower outlines, stems and tendrils.

- *Stitch count: 149 x 134*
- *Design Size: 11 x 9¹/₂in (28 x 24cm)*
- *16 x 14in (41 x 35.5cm) 14 count Aida fabric*
- *Two skeins blue/grey Anchor or DMC stranded cotton (floss)*
- *One skein of each of the other colours of Anchor or DMC stranded cotton (floss) as listed in the colour key*

1 Before you start stitching, read through the preparation instructions on page 122 to find out how to mark the centre of your fabric.
2 Following the chart on pages 108 and 109 and starting at the centre, work all the cross stitch and back stitch of the lettering using two strands of thread. See the stitch instructions on page 122.
3 Next, work all the cross stitch of the border and flowers using two strands of thread.
4 Use one strand of thread to work the remaining back stitch.
5 Using one strand of thread, work the French knots following the stitch instructions on page 124.

MOUNTING AND FRAMING
Read the hints on page 125 for help with mounting and framing. We have chosen pink and wine for our double mount, but two shades of blue or two shades of green could look equally effective.

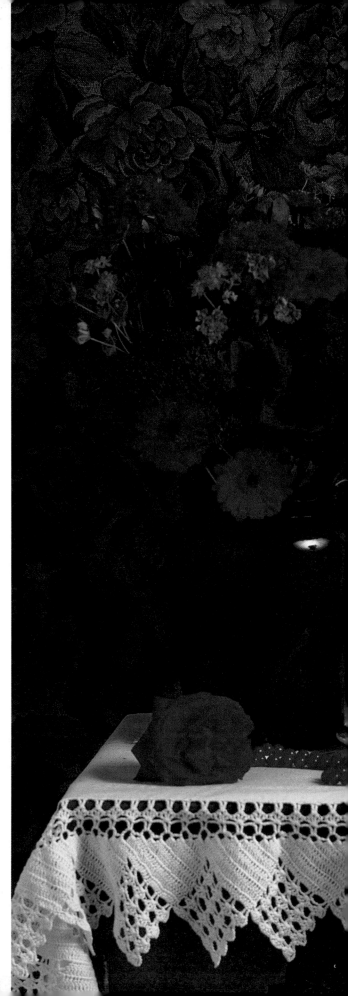

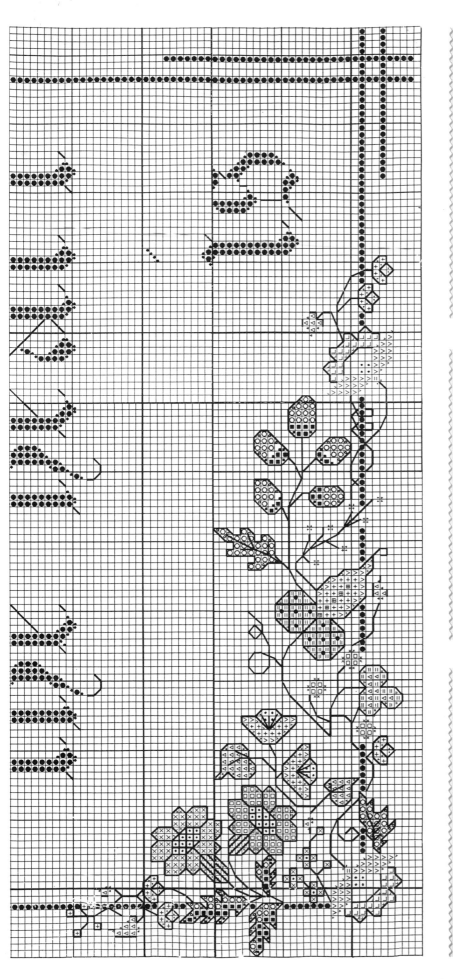

Large dark green leaves,
mauve-centred flowers, inner
outline of rose petals,
pink flowers   Wine (70, 915)
Outer edges of rose petals   Medium pink (895, 223)
Forget-me-nots   Medium blue (137, 798)
All other outlines   Dark green (879, 500)

FRENCH KNOTS
All French knots   Dark green (879, 500)

• Yellow	300	745
□ Mauve	109	210
⊞ Wine	70	915

OUTLINES, WORKED IN BACK STITCH
Lettering (two strands), large
mauve flowers, large blue
flowers (one strand)   Blue/grey (922, 930)
Acorns and stems, olive green
and light brown leaves and
stems   Olive green (846, 936)

COLOUR KEY	ANCHOR	DMC
● Blue/grey	922	930
+ Dark pink	896	3721
V Medium pink	895	223
L Light pink	48	963
X Medium blue	137	798
= Light green	241	704
△ Dark green	879	500
■ Olive green	846	936
○ Light brown	373	437

THE
COMPLETE · HOUSE
WALL-HANGING ·
· Chapter Seven ·

Creating your own Victorian Home in cross stitch pictures builds up a fascinating story, room by room. Add the family and the servants, and it begins to come to life, telling tales of people who lived amidst such sumptuous splendour, and those who worked hard in more austere surroundings. But why not take the story one step further: combine the rooms into the actual house, producing a wall-hanging of great dramatic effect, a captivating way to display your work (see pages 116–117).

Our wall-hanging opens up to view a slice of Victorian life, much as a treasured doll's house would. Doll's houses (or 'baby houses' as they were sometimes called) are now mainly thought of as children's toys; but originally they were usually made for adults. Interiors furnished with silver, ivory, alabaster and porcelain were a fashionable way to display wealth and standing, and in the nineteenth century this appealed greatly to status-conscious Victorians. The most famous Victorian doll's house, however, was probably made for children: Caroline's Cottage, built at Balmoral, no doubt provided many happy hours for Queen Victoria's children.

· STITCHING · THE · TOP · OF · THE · HOUSE ·

There are two ways of tackling the complete house. If you decide right from the beginning to commit yourself to stitching the whole house, then you could stitch it directly on to one large piece of fabric, using a large tapestry frame. Alternatively, you may prefer to make up one room at a time, and appliqué each one on to the backing fabric, see pages 116–117. If you decide to do it this way, stitch the top of the house and the nursery together on the same piece of Aida.

- *Stitch count: 280 x 140*
- *Design size: 20 x 10in (51 x 25.5cm)*
- *26 x 16in (66 x 41cm) 14 count Aida fabric*
- *One skein of each colour of Anchor or DMC stranded cotton (floss) as listed in the colour key.*

1 Before you start stitching, mark the centre of the fabric as described on page 122.
2 Following the chart on pages 112 and 113, and starting either at the centre or if you prefer at the top of the roof, work all the cross stitch using two strands of thread. See the stitch instructions on page 122.
3 When you have completed the cross stitching, use one strand of thread to work the back stitch.

4 Follow the nursery instructions on page 74 to complete the nursery design here in the roof space. Do not stitch the nursery on a separate piece of fabric.

MAKING UP
If you are stitching the house as one piece, see below. If you are stitching the rooms separately, see page 114.

· STITCHING · THE · WHOLE · HOUSE · ON · ONE · · PIECE · OF · FABRIC ·

Start by stitching the top of the house and then the nursery, adding rooms, one by one, from top to bottom.

- *Stitch count: 500 x 300*
- *Design size: 36 x 22in (92 x 56cm)*
- *42 x 28in (107 x 71cm) 14 count Aida fabric*
- *3¼yd (3m) of backing fabric measuring 39in (1m) wide. We chose a dark sage green, but any plain colour would be suitable*
- *Anchor or DMC stranded cotton (floss) in the colours listed in the colour key. Start with one skein of each colour and buy extra as required*
- *½in (1.25cm) wide wood or brass curtain pole measuring 36–40in (approx 1m) length. See Suppliers list on page 127*
- *48in (1.22m) narrow twisted cord for hanging*
- *Enough iron-on Vylene to cover the completed house*

1 Fold your Aida fabric in half down the length and mark the top centre as shown on page 122, so that the mark will show once the fabric is on your frame.
2 Attach the Aida fabric to your frame according to the frame instructions, and position the fabric so that you can start stitching from the top of the design.
3 Following the chart of the top of the house on pages 112–113, and starting from the top centre of the design, use two strands of thread to work all the cross stitch. See the stitch instructions on page 122.
4 When the cross stitch is complete, use one strand of dark grey thread (400, 317) to work the back stitch.
5 Now stitch the nursery in the attic space, following the instructions on page 74.

6 Winding your fabric on the frame as necessary, leave twelve rows below the nursery before stitching the bathroom (see chart, page 64). Line up the left side of the bathroom with the left side of the nursery.
7 Following the bedroom chart on page 50, stitch the bedroom. Line the bedroom up with the bathroom and leave twelve rows between these two rooms.
8 Continue downwards, stitching the rooms in the following order: drawing room, stairs and landing, kitchen, front door leaving twelve rows between rooms.
9 Following the brick pattern on page 114, and using two strands of terracotta thread (5975, 356), work a row of bricks down each side of the house, and another row of bricks across the bottom of the house as illustrated on pages 116–117.

MAKING UP
1 Cut the Aida fabric around the house leaving a 1in (2.5cm) margin all round. This is easy to do down the sides and across the bottom as you can follow the grain of the fabric, but take care when cutting the diagonals along the slopes of the roof.
2 Fold your backing fabric in half across the width and mark the centre of each selvedge with a stitch of thread. Open out the backing fabric and place it right side up on a work surface.
3 Cut out enough iron-on Vylene to cover the back of your Aida fabric and pin, then iron it in place on to the back of the Aida.
4 Remove the Vylene paper backing according to the manufacturer's instructions. Pin and then iron the Aida onto the backing fabric as shown in Fig 13

opposite. Machine zigzag stitch all round the Aida fabric to appliqué the house to the backing fabric.

5 Fold the backing fabric in half again across the width, with right sides together covering the Aida and matching up the selvedges. Machine or hand stitch the side seams leaving a ½in (1.25cm) margin. See Fig 14 opposite. Turn the fabric right side out.

6 To close up the top edge, hold the wall-hanging with its back towards you and fold over ½in (1.25cm) hem. Pin, but do not stitch the hem.

7 Fold over another deeper hem and pin then stitch it into place so that the row of stitching will come just above the top of the house.

8 Make one more row of stitching across the fabric approximately 2in (5cm) from the top.

9 Remove one end from the curtain pole and thread the pole through the top edge of the wall hanging. Replace the end of the curtain pole.

10 Finally, attach the twisted cord to each end of the pole either by tying it neatly or by fixing it into the detachable ends of the pole.

TOP OF HOUSE CHART

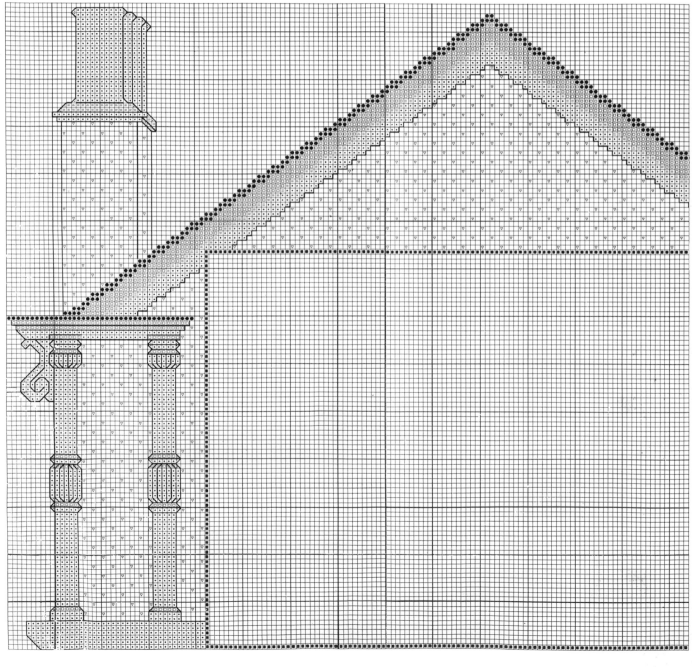

COLOUR KEY	ANCHOR	DMC
▽ Terracotta	5975	356
X Dark grey	400	317
= Light grey	399	415
● Blue/grey	922	930
• Off-white	830	3033
□ White	01	White
■ Light brown	373	437

OUTLINES, WORKED IN BACK STITCH

All outlines   Dark grey (400, 317)

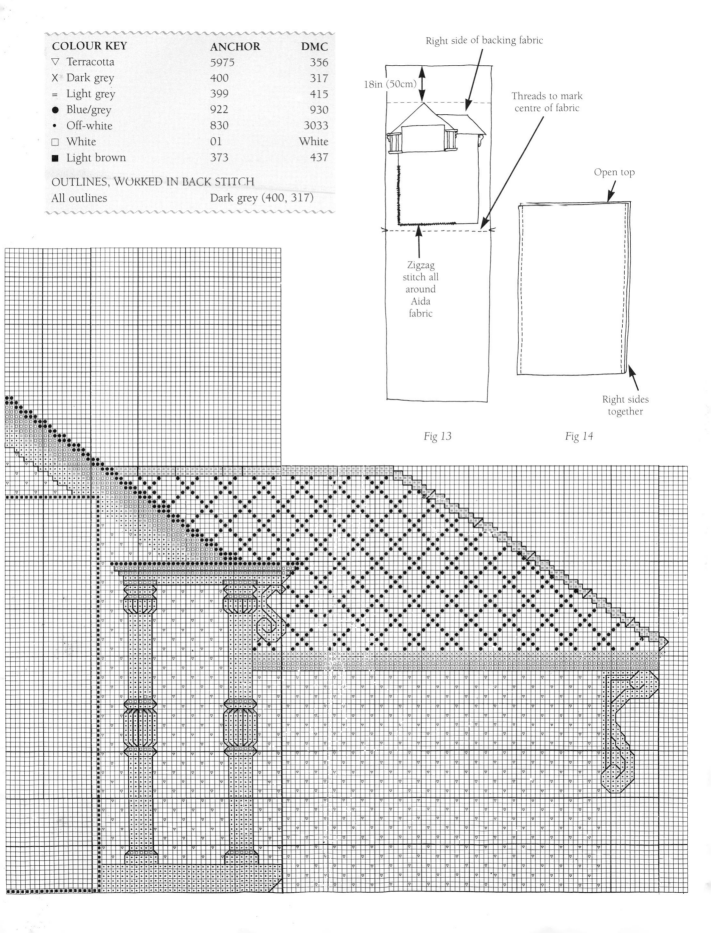

Right side of backing fabric

18in (50cm)

Threads to mark centre of fabric

Open top

Zigzag stitch all around Aida fabric

Right sides together

Fig 13   Fig 14

· ASSEMBLING · THE · WHOLE · HOUSE · STITCHED · IN · SEPARATE · PIECES ·

 In many ways it is easier to stitch the house a room at a time and then individually appliqué each picture to the backing fabric. The materials required, other than the Aida, are exactly the same as described above.

1 Stitch the top of the house and the nursery together. Stitch the other rooms individually, following the instructions in each appropriate chapter.

2 Cut down the fabric around each room picture leaving a border of about 1in (2.5cm), and be prepared to trim this down a little more if necessary to help your jigsaw of rooms to fit together.

3 The complete house is going to occupy exactly the same position on the backing material as shown in Fig 13, page 113, so lay out the individual rooms on to the backing fabric as illustrated, following the arrangement in Fig 15 opposite. Don't worry if they do not fit together exactly; simply adjust the space you leave between the pieces so that the sides of the house are straight.

4 Cut out two strips of Aida fabric measuring 30 x 2in (77 x 5cm), and another strip measuring 11 x 2in (28 x 5cm). Following the brick pattern below right, and using two strands of terracotta thread (5975, 356), work the brick pattern down the centre of each of these strips.

5 Place the strips of brick pattern down the sides and across the bottom of the house, cutting them down a little if they are too big. Pin all the individual pieces of the house to the backing fabric. The pieces should fit together with a little space between rooms as shown in Fig 15.

6 The instructions are now exactly the same as for making up the wall-hanging described on pages 112–113, except that instead of having to appliqué one large piece of Aida to the backing fabric, you can work on one small unit at a time, attaching each piece of Aida with iron-on Vylene and machine zigzag stitch. Follow the instructions on pages 112–113 to complete the wall-hanging.

COLOURS FOR THE WHOLE HOUSE

All the colours used are listed under the individual projects. However, in case you want to buy all the colours in one go, we've listed them all below, as well. Buy one skein of each to start with, and add more as necessary.

	ANCHOR	DMC
Dark green	879	500
Light green	208	563
Dark brown	381	838
Mahogany	351	400
Pinkish brown	378	407
Yellowish brown	373	437
Stone	393	640
Terracotta	5975	356
Light yellow	300	745
Dark yellow	307	783
Dark blue	149	336
Medium blue	137	798
Light blue	130	799
Palest blue	975	3753
Blue/grey	922	930
Dark grey	400	317
Light grey	399	415
White	01	White
Off-white	830	3033
Black	403	310
Maroon	22	814
Wine	70	915
Dark pink	896	3721
Medium pink	895	223
Light pink	48	963
Mauve	109	210
Peach	337	758
Gold	Cristallina, or other metallic thread	

BRICK CHART

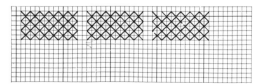

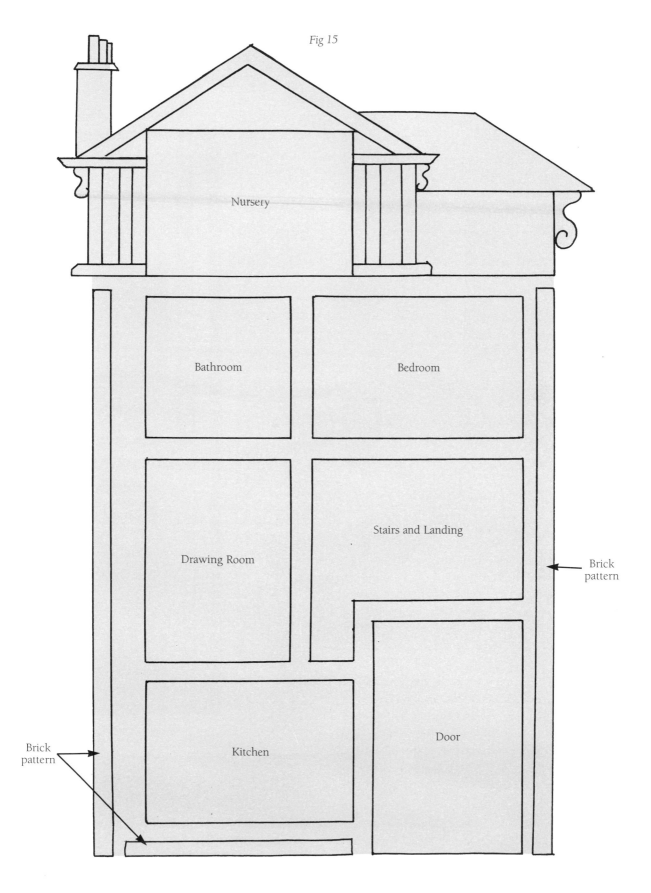

Fig 15

Nursery

Bathroom

Bedroom

Drawing Room

Stairs and Landing

Brick pattern

Brick pattern

Kitchen

Door

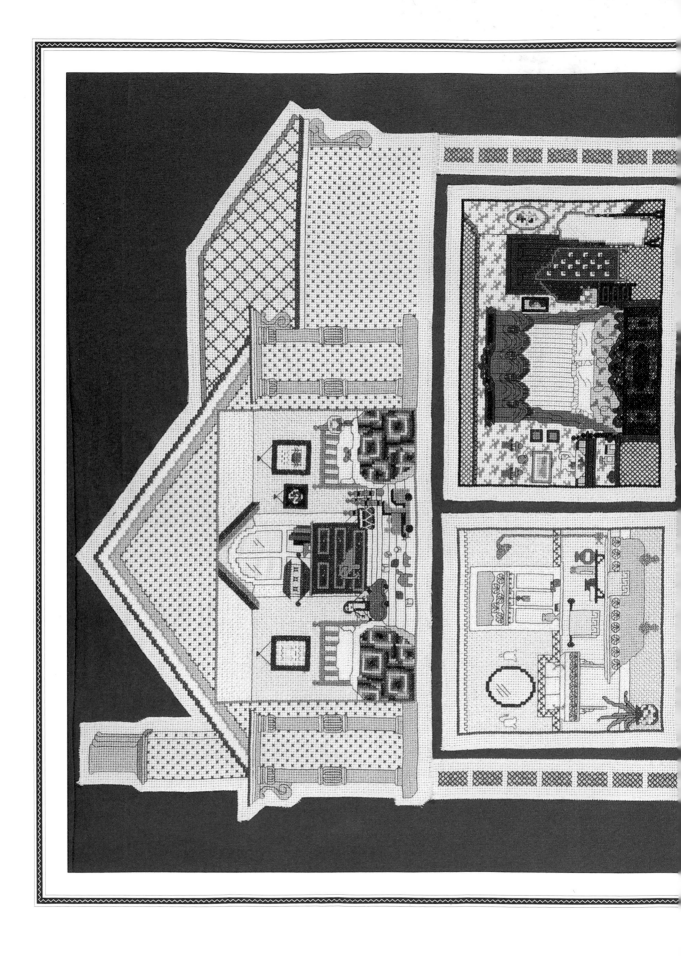

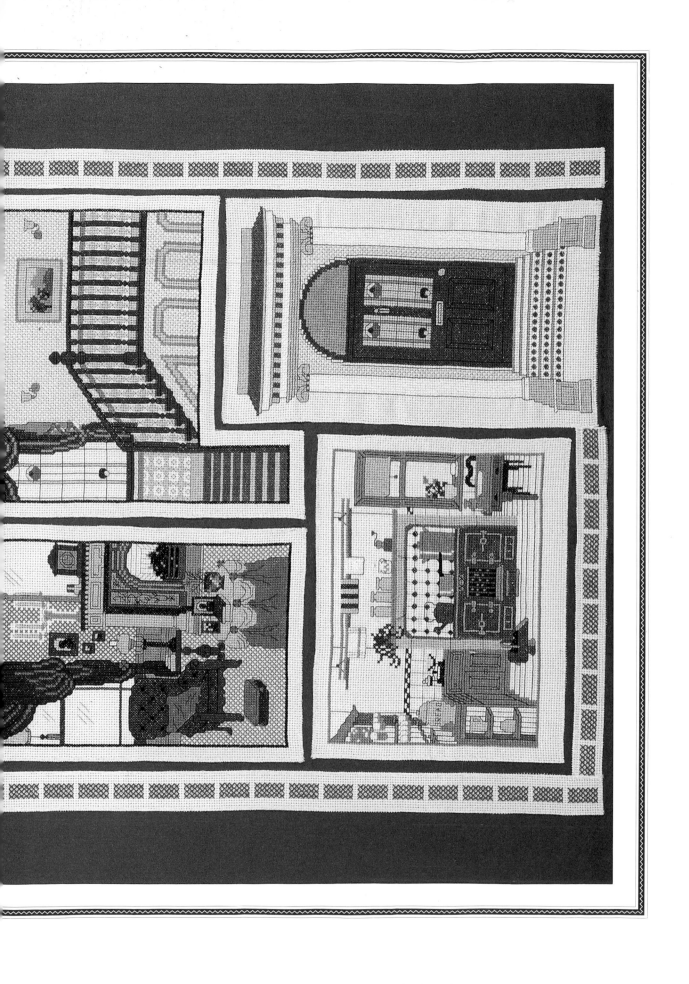

·MATERIALS· ·AND· BASIC· TECHNIQUES·

·Chapter Eight·

This chapter contains all the information you need to know about materials and techniques to work any of the projects in the book. It covers the different fabrics, threads and stitches; working from a chart; and gives hints on mounting and framing.
We all have our own ways of doing cross stitch, some of us having developed a style which suits us but which may differ from a text book description. Provided that the end result is neat and attractive it doesn't matter if your techniques vary from those of other people. For example, some people prefer to use a frame, whilst others do not; some stitch from right to left, whilst others prefer to start from the top and work downwards. So we are not going to dictate to you the rights and wrongs of cross stitch, but what we will do is show you some basic techniques from which to develop your own style. If you are already a proficient cross stitcher, you may only need to dip into this chapter from time to time if you get stuck.

· CHOOSING · AND · USING · FABRICS ·

 There are several different types of fabric you can use for cross stitch in a wide range of colours and stitch sizes. What these fabrics have in common is regular spacing of warp and weft threads to provide you with the necessary surface on to which you can sew evenly spaced and evenly sized crosses. The three main types of fabric are blockweave, evenweave and canvas.

BLOCKWEAVE OR EVENWEAVE
Blockweave is probably the most widely used fabric for cross stitch. It is woven to give the appearance of squares or blocks on its surface, making it particularly easy to sew, as one block represents one square on the chart from which you copy the design. Each full stitch is worked over one full block (see Fig 16a). The blocks are easy to count, and you know exactly where your needle should go next. Most projects in this book use Aida fabric, a universally popular cotton blockweave.

Many suppliers and stitchers refer to Aida as even-weave, but strictly speaking an evenweave fabric has a linen-like appearance, in which the warp and weft threads are evenly spaced and not grouped together to form blocks. The cross stitches are made by working over the warp and weft threads. Stitching across one warp and weft thread at a time will result in very small fine stitches. To make larger stitches you simply have to stitch across two warp and weft threads for each cross (see Fig 16b). A popular example of this type of fabric is 27 count Linda. If you prefer the linen look, but would like your pictures to work out the same size as ours in this book, then 27 count Linda would give the desired effect, provided that you remember to work each cross stitch across two warp and weft threads.

We have used cream coloured fabric throughout, but there are many other colours to choose from. Your specialist needlework supplier can advise you when you are making the choice.

Fig 16

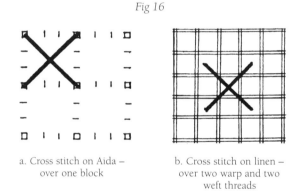

a. Cross stitch on Aida –
over one block

b. Cross stitch on linen –
over two warp and two
weft threads

CANVAS

For projects where you want to work in wool (yarn), such as furnishings like our cushion on page 52, you should use canvas which is a much stiffer type of evenweave. Again it comes in various gauges or stitch counts and with double or single interlocking threads. Your supplier will advise you when choosing, but for our cushion we recommend 10 count single interlock canvas.

STITCH COUNT

Whatever type of fabric you decide to use, you will need to know its stitch count, that is the number of stitches per inch that the fabric enables you to stitch; and this depends on the thickness and structure of its warp and weft threads.

Apart from the tiny projects such as cards and brooches and the large cushion, which is on canvas, we have recommended the use of Aida 14 count fabric throughout the book. This has 14 squares to the inch along each row, so you can sew 14 stitches each inch. It is a size that most people can see to stitch comfortably. However, you may prefer to use 16 or 18 count Aida, that is 16 stitches to the inch or 18 stitches to the inch. If you do use a higher stitch count fabric then your finished design will be smaller but finer, as each stitch is slightly smaller than with a 14 stitch count.

WASTE CANVAS

Waste canvas is a very useful tool for transferring cross stitch designs on to non-evenweave fabrics which would otherwise be unsuitable for cross stitch. It is a fine weave canvas and comes in different stitch counts like Aida fabric. So, for instance, you can buy a 14 or 18 count waste canvas, meaning that you can make 14 or 18 stitches to the inch respectively. We have used waste canvas for some of the projects in this book, for transferring small designs on to such things as pillow cases, place mats and napkins. It is simple to work with and should be used as follows:

1 Count the number of squares length and width that your design covers and cut out a square or rectangle of waste canvas sufficient to leave a couple of squares border all round your design.

2 Mark the centre of the waste canvas in the usual way as described on page 122.

3 Place the waste canvas in position on the fabric on which you are going to stitch, and pin then tack (baste) it in place round the outer edge of the canvas.

4 Work the cross stitch design as instructed, making sure that you stitch right through the two layers (waste canvas and lower fabric). See the illustration on page 120.

5 When you have completed the design, use a pair of tweezers to gently pull out the waste canvas a strand at a time starting at one edge. This is quite time consuming, but well worth the effort and care. Some makes of waste canvas recommend that you dampen the canvas before pulling out the strands to dissolve the starch that holds the canvas together, making it easier to remove. Your supplier will advise you on this.

6 Once all the strands of waste canvas have been removed, gently press the fabric on the reverse side with a warm iron.

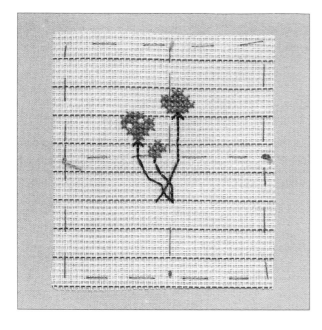

Use waste canvas to cross stitch on non-evenweave fabrics

FABRIC EDGES

You will find when handling blockweave and even-weave fabrics that they fray very little. To begin with however, you may wish to oversew the fabric edges or bind them with masking tape to prevent any fraying. If you use a rectangular frame, hem the fabric to stop it fraying when you lace it to the frame.

USING A FRAME

Traditionally, cross stitch was worked on a hoop or frame. This had the advantage of holding the fabric taut and helped to keep it clean. For many types of embroidery a frame is essential as without one the uneven tension of the stitches would pull the fabric out of shape. But the joy of cross stitch is that the stitches have an even tension and therefore do not distort the fabric. The main advantage of not using a frame is that you can stitch in and out with the needle in one go, so that you are always working with the needle and thread on the top of the fabric. Also, it's a lot easier to carry around with you without a frame. So the choice is yours.

If you decide to use a hoop, make sure that the whole area being worked fits within it. Moving the hoop over areas already worked can flatten or distort the stitches. If you don't use a frame of any kind, fold the fabric over in your holding hand so that your thumb is in contact with the back of the fabric, thus keeping the front clean. If, during the course of your stitching, you get the fabric dirty, it's a simple job to wash it when you have completed the design. Aida fabric can be gently washed by hand in soap flakes dissolved in luke warm water. Don't worry about colours running. The reputable brands of thread which we recommend in this book are colour-fast. After rinsing, roll the fabric in a towel to remove the excess water and then dry it flat. It can then be ironed on the reverse side while damp. The fabric, which may have become soft with handling, will resume its former shape and stiffness with ironing.

· THREAD ·

Cross stitch can be worked in many different types of thread, but the most commonly used is stranded cotton (floss). It can be done very successfully with wool (yarn) on canvas (see our cushion on page 52), but mainly in this book you will be using cotton threads on cotton fabric. The threads that are normally used are the six-stranded embroidery threads (floss), often called 'silks'. They are in fact cotton. The strands are sepa-

rated to give a finer effect, and we tell you how many strands to use for each type of stitch in each individual project.

Two of the leading brands of thread in the UK are Anchor and DMC. Colour references are given for both in each project. The colours of the two brands do not correspond exactly but have been chosen to tone with other colours from the same range in each case. It is therefore recommended that you stick with one brand of thread or the other. However you don't need to stick religiously to the colours we have selected, and if you are a keen stitcher you will probably find that you have many suitable colours among your own collection.

WOOL (YARN)

Working with wool (yarn) is quite different from working with cotton (floss). Canvas is a very hard fabric through which to stitch, and wool (yarn) is softer and more easily broken than cotton (floss). Tapestry wool (yarn) has been specially spun for repeated travel through canvas, and knitting wool (yarn) is not a good substitute as it is less strong and will not last. There are two main types of tapestry wool (yarn): stranded, which can be separated and stitched as one, two or three strands; and unstranded, which is thicker three or four ply wool (yarn) which can't be separated. Paterna and Appleton supply the stranded wool (yarn) which we recommend for our cross stitch cushion on page 52. However, if you would prefer to use the single thickness tapestry wool (yarn) by Anchor or DMC, simply work the cushion in tent stitch (as described in tapestry books) for a similar thickness and appearance in the finished work.

A frame is essential for achieving a neat result when stitching wool (yarn) on canvas, despite cross stitch having an even tension. Ask your local supplier for help in choosing a frame. There are many on the market, some hand-held and some free-standing, and the prices vary tremendously depending on strength and durability as well as size. See the Suppliers list on page 127.

All the advice given in this chapter on the techniques of cross stitch apply similarly to wool (yarn) work, and when you come to choose materials your specialist needlework supplier will be able to help.

METALLIC THREAD

There are many metallic threads on the market. Some unravel as you pull the thread through the fabric because the metallic covering has a tendency to peel off from the nylon or polyester underneath. The one we find easiest to use is Cristallina from Coats Anchor. It is extremely fine, so we often use three strands in the needle as we stitch. There are others, mainly Japanese and American, which are expensive, but very effective used in small quantities.

TAPESTRY NEEDLES

Tapestry needles differ from usual sewing needles in that they have a fairly large eye to take multiple strands of embroidery thread or wool (yarn), and a comparatively rounded point to slide through the holes in the fabric rather than puncturing the material. The thickness of the needle is determined by a number. The higher the number, the finer the needle. For cross stitch it is best to use a fairly fine needle, size 24 or 26.

· WORKING · FROM · A · CHART ·

For each of the cross stitch projects in this book you follow the design from a chart. This is presented in the form of graph paper with symbols in the squares to represent colours. As Aida fabric is thought of as being divided into blocks, it is easy to see that your job is to work stitches on to the blocks on the fabric so that they correspond to the marked squares on the graph paper chart. The suggested thread colours are shown by symbols and a key to these is provided in each case.

To find the centre of the design on a chart, count across to the middle point on each edge. Follow the grid lines to the middle to find the centre of the chart. This point should then correspond with the centre point which you have marked on your fabric (see page 122). It is usually recommended that you start stitching at the centre to make sure that your design fits centrally onto the fabric.

Back stitch is indicated on the chart by straight lines, and French knots are indicated by dots.

MARKING THE CENTRE OF YOUR FABRIC

The first step is to find the centre of your fabric by folding the fabric in half, and then in half again (Fig 17 right). You can make a stitch with coloured thread at the centre point on each of the four sides (Fig 18 below). As long as you start stitching from the centre of your material and as close to the centre as possible on the chart, then your picture will sit squarely on the fabric, leaving an equal border on all four sides.

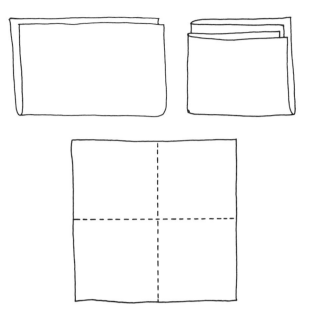

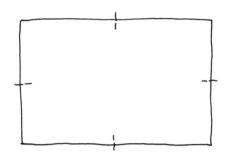

Fig 18 Marking the sides of a piece of fabric

Fig 17 Finding the centre of a piece of fabric

• WORKING • THE • STITCHES •

The following describes working cross stitch on Aida. If you want to work on Linda or other linen-look fabrics, a block equals the square made by two warp and weft threads. See Fig 15b, page 119.

CROSS STITCH

To sew a single cross stitch bring the needle up through the material at the bottom left of where the stitch is to be. Cross diagonally over one block and insert the needle down through the top right corner. Now bring the needle up through the material in the bottom right, and cross over diagonally to put the needle down through the top left of the block (Fig 19).

To sew a row of several cross stitches next to each other, starting from the left bring the needle up through the bottom left of the first block and down through the top right to create the first half of the stitch, then repeat this for the next stitch, and so on (Fig 20). When you have completed the required number of stitches in a row come back along the row completing the second part of each stitch, bringing the needle up through the bottom right and back down through the top left (Fig 21). Working a row in this

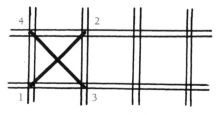

Figs 19 How to work a single cross stitch

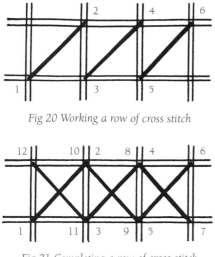

Fig 20 Working a row of cross stitch

Fig 21 Completing a row of cross stitch

way helps you to develop a regular even rhythm in the stitches. However, there are many among us who still prefer to work each complete cross stitch individually before going on to the next one.

The secret of keeping the stitches even and neat is to follow exactly the same pattern for each stitch so that the threads lie evenly on the fabric and the top stitches slope in the same direction. This explains why it is not advisable to stitch along one row and then turn the fabric upside down and stitch back along the next row. Several rows stitched in this way result in a 'ploughed field' appearance, with the threads lying differently from row to row. Keeping the tension firm but not too tight is also important. The stitches should lie well on the fabric and not pull. With practice this can easily be achieved.

DIAGONAL HALF CROSS STITCH (THREE-QUARTER STITCH)

This stitch goes under various names but is shown clearly in Fig 22. It is used to achieve finer detail, for example on curved edges. You will need to use this stitch when the colour symbol appears in the corner of a square on the chart rather than in the centre of the square.

The first part of the stitch is formed by bringing the needle up through one corner of the block (the corner in which the symbol appears) and putting it down through the centre of the block. The second part of the stitch is then formed in the normal way, by crossing from corner to corner.

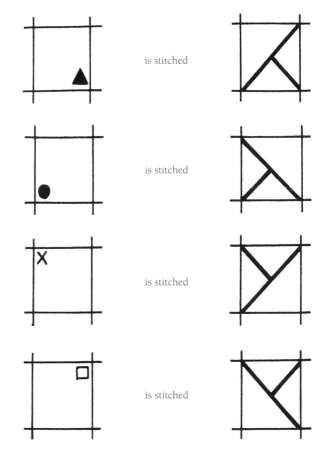

is stitched

is stitched

is stitched

is stitched

Fig 22 Diagonal half cross stitch (three-quarter stitch)

BACK STITCH

The other stitch that is used in conjunction with cross stitch is back stitch. This is used selectively to clarify fine detail and give an outline. Following Fig 23, the needle is brought up at 2 then down at 1. Next, the needle is brought up at 3 and down at 2; then up at 4 and down at 3 and so on.

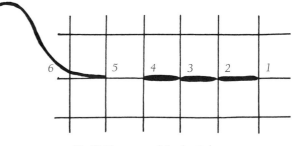

Fig 23 How to work back stitch

Stitchers often ask us how to make back stitch look neat, as it seems to be back stitch rather than cross stitch that people have problems with. So here are some tips to help you achieve neat back stitching:

1 Back stitch should always be worked when all the cross stitch is completed as it lies either on top of the cross stitch or around the outside edge of the cross stitch.

2 When the back stitch needs to be worked round the outside edge of the cross stitching, guide the thread with your thumb as you stitch pushing the back stitch firmly to the outside edge rather than letting it trail untidily on top of the cross stitch.

3 As with cross stitch, use the same pattern of stitching for each stitch so that you get into an even rhythm with your stitches rather than doing an odd stitch here and there. Of course this isn't always possible, but if you are stitching a row or outlining around an object try to form each stitch exactly like the previous one.

4 Neat back stitch cannot be achieved on top of untidy cross stitch, so follow our guidelines for the cross stitch first!

FRENCH KNOTS

A few of our projects require the finishing detail of one or two French knots, the prospect of which seems to cause panic amongst many cross stitchers! So, here in step by step detail is how to achieve perfect French knots:

1 Using one strand of thread, bring the needle up through the desired hole in the material and pick up one warp thread to the right of the hole and hold it on the needle.

2 Wrap the embroidery thread twice round the needle (see Fig 24) and pull the thread taut.

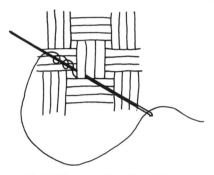

Fig 24 How to make a French knot

3 Holding the thumb over the 'knot' created, pull the needle through the knot. ·

4 Put the needle down through the original hole in the material, being careful to leave the newly created knot on the surface of the fabric.

Depending on the natural tension you use and the type of fabric on which you are working, you may find that the French knots look too small. If this is the case, work them again in exactly the same way using two strands of thread instead of one.

· STARTING · TO · STITCH ·

 To make a start, load the needle with whichever colour comes closest to the centre of the chart and make your first cross stitch, leaving a short tail of about ½in (1.25cm) beneath the fabric. Hold this under where your next few stitches will be, and work the backs of those stitches over the tail. It should hold in place without any trouble. Working outwards from the centre, change colour whenever necessary. To start another colour, work two very small stitches into the back of the previous colour of stitches. This will be sufficient to hold the thread before you start the next cross stitches.

As counted cross stitch implies, you will have to do some counting of stitches. But, provided that each new part of the design that you tackle follows on from a part you have just stitched, you can keep the counting to a minimum.

BORDERS

Having said quite categorically that you should always start stitching from the centre and work outwards, there can be some exceptions! If there is a simple border to the design, you may prefer to start with this. You can be sure of centreing correctly provided that you count up from the centre of your fabric exactly the correct number of squares as counted on the chart, and start stitching from the top centre of the border. The border stitches will have to be counted carefully, but once completed, the border makes a good reference point for starting to stitch other parts of the design.

FINISHING OFF

To finish off a colour simply make a couple of very small stitches into the back of the worked fabric. Then cut off the thread close to the fabric. Do not leave tails of thread or use knots at the back of your work because, as well as looking untidy, they can appear visible through unstitched areas of fabric once your picture is mounted on to a white backing board for framing.

· MOUNTING · AND · FRAMING ·

 Many people are not confident enough to tackle the framing of a picture once they have stitched it, and there is no doubt that a professional framer will be able to make an excellent job of displaying your needlework beautifully in whatever frame and mount you choose. But there are many ways to show off your stitching to advantage, so do not be afraid to spend some time with the framer choosing suitable colours and styles of mount and frame.

MOUNTS

A border of Aida fabric exposed around a picture is often sufficient without any mount, and a simple wood frame shows off cross stitch well. But if you do decide to have your picture framed professionally, choose a mount colour which tones with the picture and with the decor of the room in which it will be displayed. As a guideline, choose a shade of mount which is lighter than the darkest tone in your picture and darker than the lightest tone in your picture.

You can be adventurous and put an arch-shaped embroidery into an arch-shaped mount; or the aperture in the mount could be oval, circular, heart-shaped or in the shape of an initial letter. Another alternative is to have a double mount, highlighting two colours from your stitched picture. You can also choose a mount with a gold or silver line around the opening edge, to reflect the gold or silver of the frame (or the gold metallic thread used in the picture).

With needlework you can use lace or ribbon to great effect. Bows look attractive on a contrasting mountboard, while furnishing material or velvet can be used to cover the mountboard if you wish to co-ordinate with decor. An experienced framer will be familiar with all these techniques and styles, and will be happy to suggest others to suit your requirements. As far as the finished result is concerned, the choice of mount is more important than the choice of frame, as it covers more area and has a bigger impact.

FRAMES

If you are having your picture framed professionally you will be offered an enormous range of different mouldings in modern and traditional styles, colours and materials: antiqued gilts and silvers, woods, laminates, lacquers and aluminium mouldings are all possible choices for needlework.

An unmounted picture often looks better in a heavier frame, and this would certainly add to an authentic Victorian look with the room pictures in this book. Maple or stained oak frames (sometimes with a gold slip inserted in the rebate where the moulding meets the picture or mount) also have a look of period authenticity.

However, the lighter modern-looking frames can be equally attractive and may form a link between your old-fashioned stitched picture and the modern room in which you intend to hang it. So in the end it comes down to your personal choice, as there is no right or wrong way to frame your picture.

MOUNTING AND FRAMING YOUR PICTURE YOURSELF

There is a wide range of standard sized frames available for you to do your own framing and this need not be a daunting task. Cutting your own window mounts can be a bit trickier, however, so if you want to make your own mounts you may benefit from borrowing a library book on the subject first to give you the confidence to go ahead.

Aida fabric does not need to be stretched or laced on to a backing board, so provided that you buy a frame that is an inch or two bigger all round than your design measurements, you can follow these steps to simple framing:

1 Using a warm iron, gently press your stitched picture on the reverse side to bring the fabric back to its original firmness.

2 Your ready-made frame may contain a piece of white mounting board, but if it doesn't, cut a piece of white card very slightly smaller than the frame, so that it will fit snugly into the frame once the fabric is wrapped over it.

3 Fix double-sided sticky tape around the board on the reverse side, about 1in (2.5cm) from each edge (Fig 25).

4 Place the fabric, image upwards, on to the front of the board and stretch the material over the edges and on to the reverse side to press against the sticky tape (Fig 26). Take care to follow the weave of the fabric so that the cross stitch image will be straight.

5 Fix masking tape over the back to ensure that the picture is securely held.

6 Secure the picture in the frame by replacing the backing and holding it in place with masking tape if necessary (Fig 27).

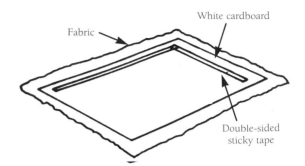

Fig 25 Place double-sided sticky tape about 1in (2.5cm) from each edge of the board

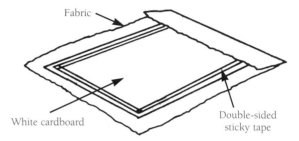

Fig 26 Fold over each edge of the fabric in turn and secure to the sticky tape

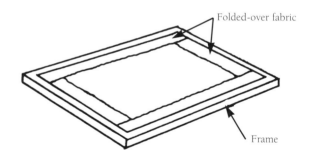

Fig 27 Place the mounted embroidery into the frame and replace the frame backing

·SUPPLIERS·

FABRICS AND THREADS
For the Aida and Linda fabrics, canvas, Anchor and DMC threads, Anchor and Paterna wools (yarns), evenweave edging ribbon and needles that we have referred to, we recommend that you enquire at your local needlework stockist. For your nearest large needlework centre or shop, look in your telephone directory under 'Art Embroidery' or 'Craft Retailers'. Any specialist embroidery retailer will stock many colours and different stitch-count sizes of fabric, as well as a comprehensive range of threads and wools (yarns), and they will be glad to advise you on choices.

WASTE CANVAS
Some needlecraft shops stock waste canvas, but if you have any difficulties you can buy it, and any other item you need, by mail order from the following shops:

Wye Needlecraft, 2 Royal Oak Place, Matlock Street, Bakewell, Derbyshire, DE4 1EE, Tel 01629 815198

Voirrey Embroidery Centre, Brimstage Hall, Brimstage, Wirral, Cheshire, L63 6JA, Tel 0151 3423514

Craft Basics, 9 Gillygate, York, YO3 7EA, Tel 01904 652840

The Stitch Shop, 29-30 The Boardwalk, Port Solent, Portsmouth, Hampshire, PO6 4TP, Tel 01705 381049

The Stitch Shop, 6 George V Place, Thames Avenue, Windsor, Berkshire, SL4 1QP, Tel 01753 858713

The Stitch Shop, Water's Edge, Brindleyplace, Birmingham, B1 2HJ, Tel 0121 6435133

FRAMES AND STANDS
Most needlework supply shops sell several types and sizes of frame, and will allow you to try them out. Some also carry the larger stands which make stitching a large piece of work so much easier. For more details contact Lowery Workstands, Grasby, Barnetby, Lincolnshire, DN38 6AW.

TOWELS FOR CROSS STITCH
Many department stores sell these towels intermittently, at very reasonable prices, so it's worth keeping a look-out for them, as they may not be there just when you want them. However, high quality towels of this type are kept in stock and are available by mail order from all three Stitch Shop outlets and from Voirrey Embroidery Centre mentioned above.

CURTAIN POLE
A suitable curtain pole for the complete house wall-hanging can be obtained from any of the larger curtain suppliers. The one we used (see page 111) is a metallic extending pole which can be adjusted to fit the width of the wall-hanging exactly.

BARBARA THOMPSON DESIGNS
Barbara Thompson Designs produce a range of counted thread cross stitch kits which are widely available. Write to Ann Green at 18 Rumbold Road, Edgerton, Huddersfield, West Yorkshire, HD3 3DB, Tel or Fax 01484 542340, for a colour brochure and stockists list.

Designs featured in this book which are also available as kits:

Victorian Conservatory
Victorian Toys – Rocking Horse
                 Doll's Pram
                 Doll's House
                 Noah's Ark
Home Is Where The Heart Is sampler
Home Sweet Home sampler
Vegetable sampler
Pincushion (in four colourways)

INTERNATIONAL DISTRIBUTORS FOR BARBARA THOMPSON DESIGNS
France, ABC Collection, 9 rue Victor Hugo, 35000 Rennes, Tel 00 33 9979 6047, Fax 00 33 9979 7354

Spain, B & M Labores, Carabela la Niña 8, 6, 2, 08017 Barcelona, Tel and Fax 00 343 280 38 62

Germany, Engbert Blok, Halsbekerstrasse 43, 26655 Westerstede, Tel 00 49 88 73 424, Fax 00 49 88 73 425

Italy, Ornaghi, Via Montello 221-223, 20038 Seregno, Milan, Fax 00 39 362 235 21

New Zealand, Broomfields, Merivale Mall, Christchurch, P.O. Box 2120

·INDEX·

Page numbers in *italic* refer to illustrations

Alphabets: back stitch, 81, 82, 86; cross stitch, 82; ornate, 85; Roman ornamental, 19
Armchair, 8
Art nouveau, 8, 50

Back stitch, 8, 11, 24, 32, 90, 102, 106, 121, 123
Bathroom, 62–71, *63, 70*
Bed, 48, 74
Bedroom, 48–61, *48*, 62
Blockweave, 118
Bookmark, 56, *58*
Brooch, 12, 14, *12–18 passim*

Candelabra, 8, 24
Cards, 13, *16*
Centre marking, 122
Chart, working from a, 121
Christmas scene, 24, *24*
Clothes rack, 30
Conservatory, 32, *32*
Cross stitch: alternate, 11, 24, 32, 62, 90; the stitch, 52, 122, 124 *see also* Diagonal half cross stitch
Curtains, 8, 11, 102
Cushion, 52, *53*

Dado, 11, 64, 102, 105
Diagonal half cross stitch, 15, 19, 50, 90, 106, 123
Distributors, 127
Door, 90, *91*
Drawing room, 8–27, *9*, 62

Egg-and-dart design, 50
Entrance, 90–109, *91*
Evenweave, 118

Fabric: Aida, 11, 18, 19, 56, 57, 118, 122, 127; canvas, 52, 119, 127; evenweave edging ribbon, 56, 127; Hardanger, 13; Linda, 119, 122, 127
Fireplace, 8
Fir tree, 24
Flowers, 12, 32, 50, 57, 106
Frame, 52, 111, 120, 121, 127
Framing, 77, 125, 126
French knots, 121, 124
Fringing, 50, 102
Front door, 91, *91*

Gardener *see* Kitchen
Greek key motif, 62, 65, 66
Greenhouse, 42

Hallway *see* Entrance
Hoop, 120
House wall-hanging, complete, 7, 110–17, *116*

Ivy, 45

Jacobean design, 50, 56, 106

Kitchen, 28–47, *28*; garden, 35; gardener, 42, *43*; gardening proverb, 45, *46*; range, 28, 30
Kits, 127

Log cabin pattern, 72

Maid, 94, *95*
Mantelshelf, 8, 28
Mats, oval and round, 15, *16*
Mounts, 77, 125

Name plates, 83, *83*
Napkins, 15, 36
Needles, 121

Night-dress case, 57, *58*
Nursery, 62, 72–89, *72, 87*

Oil lamp, 8
Outlining, 8, 19, 50 *see also* Backstitch

Panelling, 11, 102
Piano, 24
Pillow case, 15, *16*
Pin cushion, 97, *100*
Plants, 28, 32, 64
Portico, 92

Sachet, perfumed, 99, *100*
Sampler, 19, *20*, 46, *46*, 56, 75, 81, 106, *106*
Screen, 48
Shell motif, 62, 65, 66
Stained glass, 32, 90, 102
Stairs, 102, *102*
Stitch count, 119
Suppliers, 127

Tassels, 8
Techniques, 118–26
Thread (floss): cotton, stranded, 120, 127; gold, 26, 64, 69, 114; metallic, 121; tapestry wool, 52, 121, 127
Three-quarter stitch *see* Diagonal half cross stitch
Tiles, 28, 30, 62, 65, 67, 90, 97, 99
Towels, 15, 62, 65, *68*, 127
Toys, 74–81, *78, 86*

Vegetables, 36–42, *37, 41*, 94

Wallpaper, 24, 50, 102, 105
Wash-basin, 62; stand, 50
Waste canvas, 15, 36, 119, 127
Wrought iron, 32, 94